From Millie
Feb. 8, 1982

CAN I *Hope* AGAIN?

CAN I *Hope* AGAIN?

Hazel Goddard

Ronald N. Haynes Publishers, Inc.

PALM SPRINGS, CALIFORNIA 92263

Can I Hope Again?

Ronald N. Haynes Publishers, Inc.
Palm Springs, California 92263

Second edition 1981

Library of Congress Catalog Card Number 81-83582
ISBN 0-88021-022-2 (previously 8423-1445-8)

Printed in the United States of America

DEDICATION

To Bud and Joan and Ray and Jeannie....to Lee...to Linda...to all of the very fine people who have shared thier innermost problems with me, I dedicate this book. Without you I could not have known the full meaning of fear, anxiety, loneliness, confusion, despair. Nor could I have witnessed the release that comes when imprisoned emotions are set free or the restful peace that envelops the personality when the soul finds that for which it is seeking. So it is because of you I am writing this book. You have given me a compassion for those others who are suffering and cannot or will not go for help. Perhaps, in these pages, they can share the deep conflicts and experience the same release—the same hope.

CONTENTS

FOREWORD

by Dr. Paul Tournier

To write a foreword to a book on hope is an awesome task. I have been pondering it for over a month without knowing how to go about it. The problem of hope raises so many questions charged with intense emotion! It raises so many difficult questions and so many questions without apparent answers that I am fearful of hurting some readers, of troubling some, and of disappointing others. I could get out of this predicament by simply acknowledging here my very deep esteem for the author, Mrs. Goddard. Or I could refer to the friendship that links my wife and me to her and to her husband since we were guests in their home in 1961.

The friendship born that day between Mrs. Goddard and us was enhanced by our Christian fellowship. But there was even more: our collaboration in seeking a medicine for "the whole man." By this we mean that on the one hand the patient has all the technical help of medical science and scientific psychology; and on the other hand also has the personal contact and the moral and spiritual guidance which he will need to overcome the everyday problems that always compromise complete recovery and healthy development in life. This is precisely what Mrs. Goddard is trying to achieve.

For this reason I feel that it is not enough just to mention our collaboration, but I must make it available in this book. Psychology has not often dealt with hope, probably because when one speaks of hope it is hard to know whether one speaks as a psychologist or as a philosopher. We do not know exactly how to draw the line of demarcation between the psychological and the metaphysical aspect of the problem of hope and their intimate interrelationships in the total personality.

Philosophical studies have been made; theologians also preach hope. But such preaching raises many questions that are difficult to analyze from the psychological viewpoint. I congratulate Mrs. Goddard for daring to do it. It is now my turn to have the necessary courage to express my thoughts on this most difficult subject.

I think of an old friend, a well-known surgeon, in charge of a large clinic. One of his sons was eight years old when he became ill, suffering from a serious bone tumor. The disease was recent, still localized, and it had been possible to perform an extensive excision. The child seemed to be out of danger. But do we ever know? We can imagine the anxious vigilance my friend the surgeon constantly kept over his son, always looking for any signs of possible reoccurrence.

This is how all physicians secretly embrace a thousand preoccupations about their entourage and their patients. During the most simple consultation, they rapidly consider all the possibilities. To be sure not to overlook them, they consider first the most serious diagnoses. But they do not mention these because they are expected to offer hope, not anxiety. They even attempt to maintain an air of serene confidence to sustain everybody's morale.

But this is what happened: ten years after the operation just mentioned, X-rays revealed multiple widespread metastases. The father knew at once that his son was lost. What tragedy for a surgeon to feel helpless when such a beloved child is involved! How tragic the daily visits in the room occupied by this adolescent slowly on his way to death!

What aggravated the situation for my friend was that his son was telling everybody: "I am hopeful. My father will cure me." Even if the father would have found the courage to speak more openly to his son of his misgivings, that very sentence would have made such a dialogue impossible.

Years passed, painfully, after the death of the young man. One day the surgeon met one of his son's closest friends. Naturally, they talked about him and the friend revealed something that the young man had told him in confidence during his illness: "You know, I always say that I have every confidence that Papa will cure me. I only say that to please him. I know that my case is hopeless."

Here were a father and a son, one as sensitive as the other, unable to communicate freely during that tragic year of the illness! Each one was more concerned for the other than for himself, trying to help him through the crisis. Their very concern separated them, frustrating them and making it impossible for them to share their common anxiety. But what greatness in this silence, in this double silence, in this silent respect for the silence of the other!

This tragedy will lead us now, I think to the very heart of our problem. What do we really know of the hope and despair of men and of ourselves? Is there not a mixture of the two within us? When a patient speaks of confidence and hope, is it not always to reassure himself and others a little, to exhort himself not to give up hope, to overcome the menacing despair? Is he not affirming his hope as loudly as possible to silence the furtive voice of despair which is sneaking its way into his heart?

And where is the boundary between simulated hope and real hope? Could we simulate hope if there were not some authentic remnant of real hope in the depth of our person? And when a patient says his case is hopeless, is it not always just a little because he is seeking an answer to his despair through an encouraging or hopeful word? And would he even be looking for such an answer if a small flame of hope were not still burning, thirsting for oxygen in the depth of his soul?

There is not only the dialogue between the patient and doctor. There is also the dialogue doctors have with themselves. The words of hope that we speak to the patient, are we not also telling them to ourselves, to find reassurance against our own personal despair? The patient, too, is always afraid that our hope might be feigned, or that we overdo it a little to reassure him; that it is, in fact, a therapeutic hope. Surely, such an optimistic suggestion can be beneficial for a while. But it does not last.

Hear me well: I am not attempting to cast any doubt in so serious a matter upon the sincerity of our patients or our own sincerity. To the one who says, "I still have hope!" it is not proper to answer, "Are you really sure of it?" And when someone cries his despair, to tell him that there is surely still a little hope left in his heart would be to give the impression that we do not believe him, that we do not understand him, that we do not take his anguish seriously.

I do believe that everybody is sincere. But there is in the human personality an inextricable mixture of hope and despair, and we must always consider both of them together, in spite of their flagrant contradiction. Just because they may be at the same time so incompatible, they are also inseparable. And is not this interior polarity of feeling precisely the tragedy of the human condition? When we express our faith, is it not to push back the doubts that haunt us? And when we confess our doubts, is it not because there is still some faith left in us seeking to rid us of those doubts?

In organic diseases, the confidence of the doctor and his patient in the effectiveness of the cure does have an influence, but only to a certain degree. Events follow their natural sequence. Desperate patients are cured, thanks to a well-planned treatment program and the help of their own resources which the physician knows how to exploit and sustain. Yet patients animated by an undying hope may still die in spite of the best medical care and all the prayers of their loved ones.

In the case of a neurotic person and in all cases resulting from the conflicts and problems of life, like those which Mrs. Goddard describes in her book, confidence in the cure and in the therapist is even more important.

I recall a medical convention in Neuchatel where some of the most prominent psychoanalysts of Switzerland were gathered. Dr. Lingme, an adversary of psychoanalysis, suddenly asked a brutal question: "Has anyone here ever really cured an obsessive compulsive neurosis?" Old Dr. Flournoy was the only one to answer: "I think I can say that I cured one and that there was no relapse." With his usual modesty, he added: "But I do not know if it was due to my technique or to the conviction that I would succeed. It was my first case. I had come straight from Vienna. Freud had convinced me so well and filled me with so much enthusiasm that I did not doubt the successful outcome of my undertaking. In spite of my success, I was never able to handle another case with the same degree of confidence."

I have seen physicians whose power of healing diminished as their medical and psychological knowledge increased, when they discovered that things were not as simple as they had once thought. When I myself was young and did not know very much about psychology, I had results that I no longer have today.

Some compensation for me may lie in my ability to hope in spite of it and not to become easily discouraged. I have a tenacity in hoping where others, more hopeful at first in their methods, tend to give up when success is slow. Where does this perseverance come from? Some friends will probably tell me that it is the result of my faith. I do not think so. Sure, I am a believer and I always depend on God more than on myself. But many unbelievers, for instance, stoic unbelievers, are indomitable in the firmness of their hope. It seems exaggerated, perhaps even naive, to pretend that the line of demarcation in this respect is clearly drawn between the "yes" and the "no" of religious faith.

We need to go further. To do so, I will lean on the work of Professor Plugge, of Heidleberg, who made a great impression on me when I read his work in 1955 ("Uber die Hoffnung"; in: Situation I, Spectrum, Utrecht-Antwerp). The author first refers to a patient suffering from a malignant tumor. Very intelligent, duly warned beforehand of the dangers she is running by refusing to submit to radiotherapy, she maintains an invincible optimism and surprisingly accepts a vague diagnosis of osteoporosis. Does she simply pretend to believe in it? Or does she really believe it? Is she just closing her eyes to the truth? Is what is taking place in her an actual driving back into the subconscious of a reality that is too blinding? Or is she putting on a facade in an effort to spare herself and others the emotion of such tragic truth? Neither the author nor I will ever know.

Then comes the case of another patient suffering from an incurable disease. Whimsical, selfish, terribly spoiled by her husband, she had always tyrannized her loved ones. She is hopeful: her husband is rich enough to afford the best physicians. But she is impatient and anxious; she demands reassurance and complains continuously. For a long time it is impossible to tell her the truth. But one day the doctor finds it possible to tell her how seriously ill she is. It was when she understood that her case was hopeless that everything changed. All hope of a cure had vanished. "But with that," writes the author, "came another hope." Suddenly she can cope effectively with her illness. She endures her pain without complaining; she is patient, kind to the nurses, radiant. She is courageous and dies a noble death.

Finally the author refers to his talks with suicidal patients the day after they attempted suicide. Never, he says, do they refer to their gesture as a destructive act, but rather as a constructive and integrative one. One of them said, "I wanted to try this as a last resort to see if it is not possible by destroying everything to find that there is some meaning to life."

Thus, in extreme situations, when despair seems to have reached its peak, one sees another hope rising, subtle but impressive. This is what leads the author of this work to establish a fundamental distinction between common hope and what he calls genuine hope. Common hope is to hope for this or that; it has an object. It manifests a desire, a wish-fulfillment, more than a hope.

It is out of the ruins of common hope, that genuine hope is born, says Dr. Plugge. Such hope no longer has an object. When we know we are lost, we hope in spite of it. "You hope what?" someone will ask. "I don't know but I am hoping anyway." Such hope reveals itself as an inherent constituent of the inner man, independent of all object, sheltered from any disappointment. Gabriel Marcel also said: "Hope is perhaps the very substance our soul is made of."

There is a saying that goes: "As long as there is life, there is hope." It generally refers to common hope: There is yet another chance to obtain what we desire. But it can be used in an ontological sense: Hope is the very essence of life; it can only be destroyed with life itself.

Common hope is rational. It argues all the time. It weighs its chances to obtain what it desires. It relies on the science of probabilities. It computes, sometimes cheats, maneuvers, argues, pleads, or fools itself. But it does not end, for hope is never certainty nor peace.

Plugge's genuine or real hope, on the contrary, is completely irrational, vague, without desire, without object, without an argument, but peaceful. Nevertheless a link exists between the two hopes: if common hope always bounces back, if it always sprouts new leaves, it is because it draws from a hidden root, buried in the ground. Real hope is what pushes them and feeds them; this is how real hope indirectly reveals its obscure presence to the heart of all men, at the center of the person. But we only see real or genuine hope clearly in extreme situations when all this vegetation of common hope has proved inadequate. Then we go deeper.

And yet the term "real" hope is a strange one. Truth seems to apply to a reality, thus to an object. Maybe this explains why it is so fragile and so tenacious at the same time. The great paradox is that the narrow door that leads to invincible hope is the admission of defeat for a commonplace hope. We always hesitate to confess our doubts, and yet we reach the point of faith by confessing them more than by refuting them. It is also through the confession of despair that we find hope.

Thus optimists are of no use to me. They appear superficial. They are never short of arguments but they do not convince me. Christian testimonies of the type that lead one to believe that for the converted man there are no more problems, no more doubts, no more anguish, no more despair—such testimonies bother me. I am a hopeful pessimist.

But another analogy strikes me, one that will lead me to the specific domain of religious faith. There are indeed two different kinds of prayer. There is prayer which has an object, the prayer that asks for something. Just like common hope, it expresses a desire. Such a prayer is perfectly legitimate. Paul said, "Have no anxiety about anything, but in everything by prayer and supplication with thanksgiving let your requests be made known to God" (Philippians 4:6). But, just like common hope, such prayers are sometimes denied. Even in faith, our most ardent desires are not always granted.

I started to write this foreword on Good Friday and it is now Easter. I could not have chosen a more appropriate time to write these words than during the days when the whole Church is looking to the cross and to the glory of the resurrection. The cross of Christ may seem to be the "final disappointment," the supreme disappointment of the believers and even of Jesus himself: "My God, my God, why hast thou forsaken me?" (Matthew 27:46) But just exactly as in Plugge's expose, it was out of this last disappointment that there sprang an imperishable hope: *"Ave Crux, spes Unica,"* in the words of the liturgy.

Then ascends the other form of prayer, the prayer without object, without desire, the prayer of surrender: "Father, into thy hands I commit my spirit!" (Luke 23:46) In the same way, we can ardently pray for the healing of a patient and we can also, when the Spirit so guides us, simply commit this patient to the grace of God. It is God himself who brings a new hope in his revelation, a specifically Christian hope. Like the soothing hope that is born in many extreme situations, it is beyond reason; all the struggles of reason fall down before it. But now it is as if God gave back to this hope, detached of all its terrestrial objects, a new object: not any longer a thing-object, a thing we desire, partial, particular, passing; but a person, the person of Christ who opens up a new life by his death and resurrection. Thus Christian hope echoes what Plugge says of real hope, but it also adds the ultimate in meaning: on the individual level, the certainty of personal resurrection, and on the historical level, the final redemption of the world with its contradictions, and the advent of Christ.

Paul Tournier

Geneva, Switzerland

PREFACE

Truly these are fragile times and amid the stress and strain of the traffic of life, we all need HOPE.

We need HOPE to COPE— — —

Hazel Goddard has been giving that Hope to literally thousands of people throughout the nation through seminars and consultations for more than 20 years.

Her book, *Can I Hope Again?,* is an effective extension of Hazel's ministry.

She brings the hope that is from the heart of the Eternal wrapped in love and delivered in practical ways to be effective.

To God be the Glory,

Mary C. Crowley

Mary C. Crowley
President and Founder
Home Interiors and Gifts, Inc.

INTRODUCTION

Ten years have passed since *Hope for Tomorrow* first appeared in print, so I feel this new updated edition with a new title, *Can I Hope Again?* calls for a new introduction. Yet, much is unchanged. My good friend, Dr. Paul Tournier, prodded me into publishing the original work by insisting I had something to say to hurting people. During the past few years he has given me fresh encouragement by suggesting an update and revisions which may help to sharpen the focus on hope for so very many who are suffering in this increasingly troubled world. And in 1978 when I shared with him the vision of a facility in the Colorado mountains where folks could get away from stressful situations and work through their problems, he gave valuable advice and agreed to serve on the Board of Reference of the newly chartered Christian Counseling Ministries.

Ten years ago, Dr. Basil Jackson, Founder and Director of the Jackson Psychiatric Center in Milwaukee, Wisconsin enthusiastically backed the original book. His encouragement and support have continued. As vice-president of the Christian Counseling Ministries, he gives sacrificially of himself as consultant at large and as a participant in conferences sponsored by CCM around the country and more recently in the opening of an outreach in Florida.

After reading a copy of the original work, Mary C. Crowley, Founder and President of Home Interiors and

Gifts, Inc., recommended it to the vast Home Interior family across the nation and when the supply for the then out-of-print edition was exhausted, she urged me to update it and get it back into circulation.

Because my personal ministry has undergone some changes since the original work was introduced, I have added a sequel at the end of the present edition.

Hazel Goddard

CHAPTER 1

MAN—ALONE AND HOPELESS

"Is there any hope?" For nearly 24 years I have listened and watched as searching souls have asked this question. I remember the heart-broken mother whose son had become a main-liner on drugs, the shaking alcoholic who was desperately trying to stay dry, the distraught wife whose marriage was crumbling around her, the young unwed mother, the beautiful woman old beyond her years because of deep suffering from depression. The fearful, hopeless faces of these people become a passing parade as I remember them one by one. I try to remember if one of them ever asked that question and I felt there was no hope. I cannot remember a single one. So I must write about this hope—can we hope again?

Hope takes man beyond himself. It carries him into the future, whether for an hour, a day, a year, or a lifetime. It is a "for now" assurance linking him to a "for then" desire.

Does man need something beyond himself? Or does he possess inner resources to enable him to conquer tomorrow?

His conquering record is indeed impressive. The last

decade has seen more spectacular human progress than any time in recorded history. It reads like a science fiction story that defies the imagination. Man has penetrated outer space, looped around the earth, walked on the moon and sent a shuttle into orbit that landed like an ordinary airplane. all the time that the eyes of the space technicians were gazing up, another group of scientists were peering into inner space, and with dedication and genius that paralleled the outerspace spectacular, were exploring the core of the atom.

As the darkness of the unknown realities gives way to the light of man's progress, man himself has become increasingly strategic. His mind is the key to the closed doors of the unexplored wilderness of the universe. Shrewd political leaders realize this and there is intense competition to enlist the loyalty of brilliant men.

So man stands in the center of the world stage with the floodlights of his successes focused upon him—and he trembles!

The tremor goes unnoticed by the surrounding world, for it rumbles in the depths of his being. He is afraid because the intelligence that brought him success has forced him to admit that while he can penetrate space, walk on the moon, land a space shuttle, split the atom and look at its core, he has not mastered himself.

So, another search rockets ahead; man wants the formula for penetrating the mystery of his inner darkness. And as his innermost needs propel him on, his confused world shrouds his goal with hopelessness. My counseling files reveal that people are aware that they have needs they cannot satisfy. They are hurting and are asking for help. They are also disillusioned with life and some are so weary they are tempted to give up. Yet they know they would lose all hope by giving up and so they keep coming and hoping.

Is this hope an empty remedy—a tranquilizer that merely deadens the senses? Does it suspend one in an unreal world of wishful thinking?

MAN—ALONE AND HOPELESS

One of my patients said that the experience of hoping—the feeling of inner expectation—is almost better than the result of the hope. How often words of wisdom have come out of deep suffering! If what my patient said is true—and I believe it is—then there is no such thing as false hope. Hope cannot be false when its healing balm soothes the pain-wracked soul that awaits a complete cure.

If I did not believe that man needs hope because he was created with this capacity, I would believe it because of the people I have conferred with behind the closed door of my office. If I did not believe in the life-giving and soul-healing properties of hope because of its intrinsic quality, I would believe in it because of what my files tell me about people who have hoped.

In the following chapters we will share some of our life together as patient and counselor. I say "we" because in every experience related in this book I have not only the permission but the enthusiastic cooperation of those who have been involved. They do not object to sharing their suffering and they want others to know of their hope and their answers.

To imply that I have a corner on problem-solving would be naive, indeed. Rather, I identify strongly with Dr. Tournier's personal reflection in his book *Adventure in Living:*

"For me, to write a book is not to teach or to create a work of literature; it is to have an adventure in company with my readers.... It gives me that same enjoyment that is inherent in all adventure."

CHAPTER 2

DOCTOR-PATIENT-COUNSELOR TEAM

The answers to modern man's anxieties are not found in a single formula, nor are they found in the same way by different people, but if answers are found they will be discovered in the complete personality, not in a part of his being. The following story of one man's search and final discovery demonstrates how psychiatry, medicine, the patient's determination, and spiritual power worked together to bring hope, understanding, purpose, and finally, health to his life.

Bud was the first patient with whom a physician, and I (a counselor) worked together with the "whole person" concept. Because of the changes in Bud, we became convinced that our combined efforts should be extended to other patients. To put it in Bud's words—when we asked him how our treatment of his whole person differed from other methods he had tried for years—"Just one difference: results."

My first contact with Bud was at a hospital bed equipped with weights, bars, straps, and other apparatus that is used with a patient in traction.

Bud was a successful and well-to-do businessman whose life had skidded out of control in alcoholism, then through the help of Alcoholics Anonymous he had fought his way back up. But Bud had a vacuum inside with the discontinuance of alcohol, and he was a wound-up dynamo with no place to run. Periodically he became so excruciatingly tense his back had to be put in traction.

Bud had gone to a psychiatrist every week for eight years and had gained insight into his problems. Because he threw himself into everything he did, he worked diligently at therapy and rigorously followed medical advice regarding care of his body. Yet with all his progress, a gnawing emptiness tore at his insides. So Bud was still searching for an answer to his haunting loneliness.

He had complete confidence in his medical doctor, who was helping him to look at his whole person in a process of integrative treatment. One day while making her hospital rounds, she found Bud reading a Bible. Very seriously, he told her of his search for meaning to life and commented that she seemed to have found that meaning. Thoughtfully, his doctor asked if he would be willing to talk to a friend who was a counselor. "You're the doctor; if you think I need to talk to her, send her in," was his response.

Bud greeted me the next morning with, "So you're the answer girl! Well, I've got questions!"

While driving to the hospital, I had thought about possible points of contact with this patient. I must be tactful, nondirective, and must put him at ease. But Bud's direct, honest greeting put *me* at ease and I knew we would communicate.

He told me of his past life. He described his years as an alcoholic, how he was unable to cope with the mental anguish caused by the anxieties, tensions, and frustrations that are a part of an alcoholic's daily existence. He praised Alcoholics Anonymous for their help in keeping him sober.

He progressed to the place where sobriety was a habit rather than an exception. Then he made the disheartening discovery that sobriety was not the complete answer; he was sober but depressed.

Bud started searching for answers to his restlessness. He talked to priests, pastors, laymen, anyone who would talk about religion. He followed their suggestions to pray, trust God, have faith, think positively, take a day at a time, love...without success. He talked for more than an hour, painfully reliving his past. Then he reached over to his table and picked up a Bible and said, "Somehow I believe the answer is in here, but I can't find it."

I asked him what he had found since starting to read. He said he believed in the existence of God. He believed God was trying to reach him but there was a block somewhere. He knew he was missing something. He said he saw that "something" in his doctor and in me.

I was silent a few moments trying to decide the best way to help Bud find the missing answer.

"I don't get it," Bud interjected. "Is it some sort of a secret? If you know, tell me!" Again Bud's direct honesty jarred me, and I responded in the same way.

"Have you read anything about Christ?" Bud looked surprised and then remarked, "Oh, him. Yeh, he was an all right guy." Then with a questioning look he added, "But if you ask that, I must have missed something about him."

I told him I thought he had. I put a book mark in a page of his Bible and suggested he examine that passage. I knew Bud did not need my help in reading; his earnest searching would be enough.

As I got up to leave he seemed to want to talk some more, but I felt that the strain of recalling his past experiences had exhausted him. His parting words stayed with me as I drove to my office. "I didn't really get any answers, but for the first time something inside tells me I'm going to." The look of hope in his eyes told me the process had started.

CAN I HOPE AGAIN?

We hear often of the wonderful feeling of release when the patient has been able to communicate his suffering to the therapist, but little about the enthusiasm of the therapist who sees a bright look of hope on the face of a patient. Though the first surge of hope may be short-lived, the counselor feels that the negative and destructive forces of emotional illness have at least slowed and building has begun.

These were some of my thoughts as I drove fifteen miles from the hospital to my home. There was no doubt in my mind that Bud's basic need at this time was spiritual. He had learned much about himself throught psychiatry, he had learned discipline and concern for others through Alcoholics Anonymous, he had been humbled through suffering, but the core that would make all of these pieces fit together was missing. Spiritual reality is only spiritually discerned; this was no human task. I prayed.

Before I returned to the hospital the next morning, a call came from Bud's doctor. She wanted to make certain I was planning to see our patient, for he had already asked her when I would be there. "Bud has made a discovery and wants to tell you about it." There was something in the doctor's voice that told me the discovery was important.

I knew it was true as soon as I saw Bud's face: "something different" was there.

A new mellowness accented Bud's voice as he greeted me. "Will you tell me just two things? How could I be so stupid as to have missed the center of the whole thing? And why didn't anyone else tell me this?"

I did my best to explain the difficulties of seeing Christ as the hub or center of Christian understanding and pointed out that people who directed him toward God and to prayer were a part of the healing process. For, surely, if God is God he will guide the searching soul to himself. It was refreshing to hear Bud's blunt interpretation of the enlightenment he had received.

"It didn't dawn on me that there was an in-between

guy. But it makes sense. I never did understand why the cross seemed so important, but that was tied into the whole deal." If Bud's vocabulary did not reveal his reverence, the tone of his voice did. He was serious and thoughtful, however, as he expressed his doubt about God taking away all his guilt. "That's a little hard to buy at first, for a guy like me, anyway."

This was the beginning of many hours spent together. Sometimes it would be Bud and his doctor; sometimes Bud and me. Often the doctor and I compared thoughts and concepts. We learned from each other. The times when all three of us were together were particularly productive.

Just as Bud had applied himself in psychiatry and medical treatment, now he "dug in," as he put it, to "learn what God has to say about me." It was not easy for him. He had to learn that spiritual enlightenment does not immediately disperse all problems, but it throws light on them. He discovered that God does not promise freedom from illness and stress and that the Christian is no more immune to emotional or mental illness than he is to cancer or the common cold, but he is promised help and strength and he is never alone.

Only a small portion of what Bud eventually learned could be communicated by another person; Bud had to experience it. As he continued to have days of depression and anxious hours, he learned to understand the side-effects of hope and faith. After each episode his faith became stronger. Then after the process had been in operation for several months he learned the secret of abiding faith. Even though he could not *feel* God's presence, he *knew* God was there. Where a deep restlessness had pervaded his being no matter how pleasant the environment, now a solid foundation of faith and security kept him steady. Bud knew he was secure in God's love and care. He had found his true identity.

Bud no longer had tense back pain and his headaches and muscle spasms were gone. I told him about a research paper I had written and asked if he would read it. At that time, Bud was agreeing to read anything I suggested—even a research paper. The paper was entitled "The Role of Religion in Illness." During my preparation, I took notes on patients, tested various theories, changed methods, and spent hours comparing and sharing with other therapists and counselors. I selected patients I had seen at least five years previous to my research to enable me to evaluate their progress. The results of the research surprised me. I had believed strongly in the benefits of spiritual faith to a person's health, for I witnessed it daily in my office, but I had no idea it played such a prominent role. Not only did a patient's faith affect his attitude and emotions, but it often hastened the healing of physical illnesses.

Bud was impressed and enthusiastic about my findings. Again he expressed regret that he had not known all of these truths years ago. As Bud experienced these realities, his growth as a person was phenomenal. His family saw it and his friends watched in amazement. Changes appeared in Bud's thinking. He wanted to spend more time with his family. He had three teen-agers and he recognized their need for him, so he decided to "get out of the rat race" and go to Florida. Bud was about 45 and had no intention of quitting work; he just wanted to change the direction of his work.

Bud's wife was concerned about his leaving his two therapists, and we went to his home to discuss it together. We were greeted with, "Well, you two are about to open an extension department in Florida! Let's make plans!" It was obvious that Bud was ready to leave our concentrated therapy.

The story of our "extension department" in Florida could make a separate chapter. Bud was serious about his offer. Shortly after he was settled we received a call to come down and look over his set-up and make plans. So we spent ten days in his lovely, spacious home on the waterway. There was a pleasure boat and a fishing yacht. We had to spend time on both so we would know what he intended to do with the patients we sent his way. It all seemed unbelievable, but this man's enthusiasm was catching and we were caught up in it. How could we deny such complete commitment? Every morning when we arose, we found our new colleague waiting for us with books open and questions ready. His mind was like a sponge soaking up every bit of information he could get. Bud felt he was late getting started in real living and he didn't want to waste any more time. His reading involved psychological as well as religious books.

One morning he greeted us with, "It's about time you woke up; there's something here that's driving me crazy!" He held up his Bible and said, "I've found a new person in here and I don't know what to do with him. It's this Holy Spirit. I've been able to put God in his place and Jesus Christ in his but now I find this new one."

Explaining the Holy Spirit in simple terms so Bud could grasp it quickly was no easy task. He listened intently then said: "I get it. He is God's errand boy." I shivered a little as I thought what my theologian husband would say, but I felt it was more important that Bud have at least an initial answer so I agreed that his concept would do for now. I knew at the rate Bud was devouring his Bible that it would not be long until he had a more profound understanding of the Holy Spirit, and I promised to send him a book on the subject when I returned home.

Later that morning we were relaxing on his patio and I was reading Tozer's *Pursuit of God.* I put it down beside my chair and closed my eyes. A few minutes later I reached for my book and it was gone. Bud was reading it. "Where have you been hiding this one?" There was an accusing tone in Bud's voice.

I told him I didn't think he was ready for that book, but that was a mistake. Bud considered my remark a challenge and I did not see the *Pursuit of God* again until he had read it through. He ordered several dozen copies of the book and immediately sent them out to friends.

In following years, any alcoholic friend or any patient we sent to Bud was entertained and counseled by this man who had found peace of mind. As he put it—his "batting average" was good. This was particularly true in regard to alcoholics.

We kept in close touch with him. We communciated by phone and sometimes Bud would come to see us and we would visit him. One day I called him about Jan, a young woman I was counseling in marriage problems.

Jan was on the verge of filing for divorce but was able to admit that she was too emotionally upset to make such an important decision without taking time to go away and seriously think it over. She was considering Florida, so with her permission, I called Bud and gave him a brief rundown of the situation. Bud arranged a hotel reservation for Jan across the waterway from his home.

In the days that followed Bud spent many hours with Jan. She visited in his home, got acquainted with his family, went to relaxing spots in the area, and spent many hours on Bud's yacht talking about men, women, life, marriage, God..."There wasn't any important subject that was relevant to my problem that we didn't discuss," Jan told me later.

One morning as the fishing yacht pulled out of the harbor, Bud and Jan stood beside the rail and looked to the far horizon and Bud said, "Today, Jan, I would like to keep right on going and become a part of what's beyond this old world." There was no bitterness in the words, just a deep yearning for God.

Bud got his wish that day. He had just landed a blue marlin—his first. I had often heard him say, "Someday I'm going to catch one of those if it is the last thing I do." It was. With Jan and the ship's captain standing helplessly by, Bud's spirit suddenly and quietly went to his Maker as his heart stopped beating.

There was a long ride back to shore, phone calls from

the boat, a waiting ambulance, Bud's wife to console, and all the while Jan was remembering things Bud had taught her. The first thing she did when the emergency activity was over was to call her husband Bill and tell him she needed him. He came immediately and together they gave support to Bud's family and stayed with them until after the funeral.

The togetherness that Jan and Bill shared in that experience healed their wounds and today, 20 years later, they are together raising their family and benefiting from Bud's last "assignment." To us, the loss was great. We still feel it.

As I reread what I have written, I am seated on a balcony high above the shoreline in Florida. Some friends have very kindly given me the use of a penthouse apartment where I can relax and work on my book. I feel very close to my friend Bud this morning. I look down over the expanse of blue water and watch the whitecaps as they form a continuous line toward the shore. Way out, an occasional white break tells me there is some turbulence out in the deep and I think it may have been just such a morning from this same shore ten years ago when my friend headed out in his fishing yacht. I can picture Bud clearly as they pulled away from shore. I can almost hear his strong, deep voice as he said those poignant words. He loved the sea. I had been on his boat when he told me, "I hope the last assignment God has for me is out here for this is where I want to meet him."

Now, I ask myself why I have taken a whole chapter to tell about Bud. Is it because I needed to share with others what has meant so much in my life and work? That is part of the answer, but it goes far beyond that. I am anxious that you, my reader, understand what I mean when I speak of the treatment of the whole person. Dr. Tournier has used this term in most of his writing, and if you are one of his readers you already know what this includes. Many others speak of this concept, but seeing all of these different facets working together in the life of one man should give us a clear frame of reference for the experiences that follow. Together, psychiatry, medicine, theology, and human effort became a part of Bud's restoration. Together, the doctor and I fused our concepts and passed them on to Bud. Together, the three of us shared so that we all benefited and Bud joined us in passing this healing therapy on to others.

Working together provides a healing balm for weary, despairing people—and Jan and Bill are rejoined in harmony. Together, we can hope again.

CHAPTER 3

RELEASED

It was obvious that the young woman sitting beside me was desperate as she tried to describe her feelings.

"You just can't know this terrible feeling...I'm so panicked I want to run but I don't know where to go...and I can't run...it's like I'm frozen!"

She was a well-dressed, attractive, married woman. Her husband was a successful executive and they had four children. Now she sat in my office, twisting her handkerchief into knots and perching on the edge of the chair like she was ready to take off out the window.

Tears fell as she asked, "What is wrong with me? I didn't used to be like this!"

Just one week later, this same woman walked slowly into my office, sank into a chair and stared straight ahead. I asked her what she would like to talk about and she answered, "Nothing. I feel just like nothing." The week before she was suffering from acute anxiety; this week she was agonizing in a state of nothingness. Both conditions immobilized her as a person.

Apprehension, uncertainty, fear, restlessness, foreboding toward an unknown but imminent danger —

however we describe the illness of deep anxiety, or whether we think of the words associated with depression — despair, melancholia, apathy, emptiness, loneliness, nothingness — words alone cannot express the feelings of such a patient. Both of these illnesses are integrally related to the whole person.

I do not pretend to have all of the answers for the multiple problems involved in anxiety and depression. As one who has spent many hours with the anxious and the depressed, however, I have learned much about their despair, their hope, and their release.

Of all the problems and suffering of my patients which I have shared, deep depression stands out as the most agonizing, and acute anxiety as the most frightening. The deeply depressed have extreme difficulty in describing how they feel. The very nature of the illness — the hopeless, dead feeling and the frozen emptiness — prevents verbalizing. Often sufferers are locked in with their misery. How can one adequately describe the paralyzed throat, the tongue that seems so big it fills the mouth, the jaws that ache from clamped tension? Can the unreasonable fear of going to the grocery store or sitting in a church be communicated to one who has never experienced this panic? Or, how does one portray the racing thoughts that collide and tumble over each other when they refuse control and direction?

How often I have worked with a puzzled, frustrated husband to help him give his depressed or anxious wife the support she desperately needs. Husbands rarely come to an understanding, but they usually come to an acceptance and they will cooperate if they have sufficient faith in the counselor.

In this state of emotional illness more than any other, the patient needs to know hope. But how can one hope in the midst of hopelessness?

There is no fool-proof formula. To give a pat remedy would repel the patient and drive him deeper into his despair or panic. Just as getting caught in the tangled bonds of anxiety and depression is a process, so is coming out a process. It involves patient and counselor in a goal-oriented, structured schedule. It is painstaking work that pays rewarding dividends for both patient and counselor.

In this state of emotional illness, the patient often needs the supportive role of the counselor. In frightening panic or abject despair, the patient can know that there is one person available at all times who understands. In these cases, I have often disregarded some of the "do's" and "don'ts" of my training. Whether I allowed "over-dependence," played the "mama role," or was "too direct" seemed unimportant when I knew my patients needed to lean on me.

Lest I be misunderstood, I add that I strongly believe in the responsibility of the patient. I abhor the debilitating weaknesses and unnecessary regressions that accompany unwise counselor-patient relationships. But there are times when the anxious and depressed patient needs to be met where he is. In such situations mistakes may be made. The honest counselor then makes an honest admission and goes on.

I recall a woman patient I had in goal-oriented therapy for six years. Ann is a middle-aged, unmarried, intelligent woman who, because of a very low self-image and a deep sense of insecurity, lived from one hour to the next in an acute anxiety state. She was afraid of her father, afraid of her brother, afraid of the neighbors. She was in constant dread of facing the public in any way. She could not go to a grocery store, a dress shop, a doctor's office without acute panic. She never went out alone — always with her mother. After she had been a medical patient in the clinic for many years, she was referred to me and in the first interview she sat huddled in a chair looking at her hands.

Sessions had to be short at first, with the only goal being to establish rapport and confidence. Gradually she began to look up at me and to talk. There were weeks of gentle acceptance and guidance as she began to talk about her fears, her disappointments in herself, her weaknesses – always negative, down-grading comments about herself. I had goals for her but did not dare tell her about them yet. I knew she had to be slowly weaned away from her mother; I knew she needed to become aware of her own strengths and to use them. It was a slow process.

Specific milestones stand out as I review her story. There was the time she needed teeth pulled. The very thought of the dentist chair petrified her. We hospitalized her and I went to the hospital with her instead of her mother. That was the first time she had been away from her mother for years. How proud she was when it was all over! Then there were our trips to the dress shop, the shoe store, the grocery store – all without Mother.

Next she needed to go alone. She was sure she could never do this. There was a little grocery store down the street and we talked about her going for a loaf of bread. She tried several times but would get part way and have to turn back. One day I was called to the phone and an excited voice told me: "I made it, Mrs. G! I made it! I bought the loaf of bread! I'm weak but I feel great!" The process was well underway, and each time a step was made her hope grew stronger.

One day I asked Ann if she would like to join our group of women. She resisted at first, but finally said she'd try. She sat beside me for several sessions and then as she felt accepted by the women she was able to sit anywhere in the room. But she said nothing. At times I could tell that she had something to say – like the morning one of the other women was sharing her hostility toward her brother. I looked at Ann as I asked the group how they felt about what had been said. Ann's hostile eyes met mine and she blurted out, "Men! They're all alike!" then put her hand to her mouth and gasped, "I talked!" That did it. The women responded and from then on Ann was a part of the group.

Next on the goal agenda was learning to drive. The very suggestion of it threatened Ann so much she tried hard to regress, but contact was made with a drivers' school, an understanding woman teacher was selected, and in three months Ann had her driving license and a car.

Later, when her father was in a rest home, Ann could drive to visit her father regularly. Going to see her father brought ambivalent but meaningful feelings to the surface. Many counseling sessions were involved in dealing with these feelings. I asked her once if she ever kissed her father when she went to see him She gasped, "*Kiss* him! Why, he'd shove me away." I said nothing, but her eyes met mine and she got the message.

The next week her first words were, "I kissed him."

I asked, "Did he push you away?"

"No, tears rolled down his cheeks and he squeezed my hand." There was a new softness about Ann. It was a real breakthrough.

Growth experiences have continued for this patient. She has worked hard in therapy. There have been periods of depression, panic, and regression, but after each setback more progress is obvious. At this time, her father and mother have died. She sees me only on occasion.

It was while in the group that this patient found she could trust God. She first had to learn to trust a person, then a group, next her father, and then she could respond to God.

My experience with the emotionally ill has convinced me that there are times when it is impossible for a patient to trust God or to receive spiritual therapy until he first receives emotional help. Such was the case with Ann. Now dependence upon God is part of her daily life.

Goal-oriented therapy is not always as obvious as it was in Ann's case, but some structure and goals are always needed for the patient to break the vicious and frightening patterns of anxiety and depression.

How does a woman who is terrified of air travel and

yet feels guilty each time she refuses to go with her husband break the pattern? Regardless of the type of therapy she is receiving, does the day come when she must board a plane and fly? One of my patients had not been on a plane for eight years. As a part of her therapy, a flight was scheduled, then another and another. Now she is glowing with the release she feels. She knows there may still be times of panic, but she believes she can cope because she *did* cope.

How about the housewife who is immobilized because of depression? Looking at her ill-kept home and children overwhelms her with guilt and drives her deeper into depression. How will she break through the darkness? Is medication the answer? Will regular visits to the counselor's office accomplish it? Of course, these are a part of her treatment. But will there be a day when she must begin to function? Sometimes I have given such patients specific lists of simple tasks. One told me of angrily ripping it up and then piecing it together to see what she should do first. Another told me of tears dripping into the dishwater as she doggedly followed my schedule.

I told one woman I did not want to see her the next week unless her curtains were washed and ironed. Each week for months she had bemoaned the fact that along with the rest of her dirty house her curtains were "filthy." She went out angry and stayed up all night washing and ironing her curtains. She began to function in her home again. I was dismayed later when she invited me to her home and I found that each room in her eight-room house had organdy curtains! I had neglected to find out how many curtains she had before making my demand.

Since goals are needed for treating the symptoms of emotional illness, certainly the patient needs the counselor's direction in understanding and coping with the basic causes of his illness.

Of the numerous basic factors that cause illness, guilt stands high on the list — some professionals put it first.

The discussion of the problem of guilt and its cure could make a book in itself, and many volumes have been written on this subject. From the perspective of whole-person treatment, Dr. Paul Tournier's *Guilt and Grace* is first on my list. Here I will consider guilt only as I have viewed it with my anxious and depressed patients and as it involves goal-oriented therapy.

Guilt is real; guilt is also false. The only way to reconcile those two assertions is to realize there are two kinds of guilt. Can both types receive the same basic treatment? I believe so. Whether guilt is actual or false, it is only fair to confront the patient with reality when he is psychologically able to accept reality. Does this confrontation assure acceptance, and does acceptance guarantee freedom from guilt? I have not found it so.

I had a patient who was referred to me with a post-partum psychosis. She was a practicing psychologist and had been under seven years of psychoanalysis herself. She knew why she reacted the way she did. She accepted her strengths and her weaknesses objectively, but she had never lost her sense of guilt. She drove sixty miles twice a week to our clinic. One day she said she had asked herself on the way home from her last conference why she came all that distance because she had not learned any more about herself. But, she said, she *felt* something each time that she had never felt before; it was hope.

As we discussed her whole person, including her spiritual needs, the process that started with the feeling of hope grew to include knowledge of the true guilt in her life. She had never been able to resolve her guilt because she had considered it all pathological and would not face it. As her knowledge of spiritual truths grew and she understood and accepted the atonement of Christ for her, the real guilt was dissolved.

If true guilt cannot be resolved by treating it as pathological, can pathological guilt be removed by treating it as real guilt? How often well-meaning pastors will tell a guilt-ridden parishioner to "pray about it," and despite the prayers of the troubled person, the pastor, and the congregation, the one suffering pathological guilt is driven deeper into his guilt. Since God "did not answer," he must be beyond help.

Pathological guilt is obvious in the expression, "I believe God forgives me, but I cannot forgive myself." I have heard this so often from Christians that one of the first statements I make to a patient who has experienced conversion is: "God has forgiven you; now forgive yourself. God has accepted you; accept yourself." It may take months of therapy before the patient can truly accept himself, but if he is told simply to pray without being given psychological help he may never enjoy the peace and freedom offered him by God.

Does this limit God? How can God be limited? He works mediately and immediately, and finite beings cannot regiment the infinite. I have seen miracles of God in the personalities of my patients, but usually it involves a process. Does this diminish the miracle? I believe not. While treatment involves a process, the results are sometimes more immediate. An experience I had with an acutely depressed hospital patient illustrates this.

I had never seen this woman before I was asked to visit her. Daily hospital care and medication had failed to alleviate her acute depression, and my visit was to be a last effort before transferring her to a mental hospital.

When I arrived the patient was sitting at a table, starring at pieces of a jig-saw puzzle. I introduced myself, and the patient, without looking up, acknowledged my presence in a hollow, meaningless tone: "You're the one who's supposed to help me."

I sat down across the table from her. I picked up a piece of sky and put it in place. We sat silently working the puzzle for a while, then I noticed her prayer beads lying on the floor. I picked them up, and as I did she said, "They don't do any good—God doesn't care." I told her I thought he did. She asked why, and I told her because the Bible says so and I believe the Bible.

"Then why won't he help me—especially at night? I feel so alone...then I am afraid...my mind races...I can't sleep...it is hell." The tone of her voice had changed from a monotone to a quivering cry.

I asked her if she had read where God promises peace. She shook her head. I gave her the words slowly: "Thou wilt keep him in perfect peace whose mind is stayed on thee." I asked her to repeat them. She tried, but could not remember more than two or three words. I wrote them down on a small slip of paper and gave it to her.

The next morning I met her doctor in the hospital corridor and she told me that our patient had improved and would not be transferred. She asked me what had happened in our conference. I told her I was not sure but suggested we go see the patient.

I was not prepared for the transformation. The patient I had seen the day before was a deeply depressed pre-psychotic woman. The one who greeted me now was smiling and in solid contact with reality. She reached in her robe pocket and brought out a small, crumpled piece of paper.

"This is what did it! In the night every time I felt that awful aloneness and panic, I read this. I'll bet I read it a hundred times, then I fell asleep with it in my hand, and this morning it is like a curtain has lifted."

Was it magic? Power of suggestion? Mental concentration? Positive thinking? Any number of tags could be put on what happened that night in Room 221. Many factors no doubt were involved, but behind it all was the power of God and his promise of peace. I believe that. The doctor believes it and so does our patient.

Was her healing any more real than Ann's? Did it lack process? How can we know? Was it the Scripture portion alone that healed? How about the preceding hours of help given by her doctor before I came?

CAN I HOPE AGAIN?

We cannot judge or bind God's power by our limited knowledge. Isn't this one reason why we can have hope?

The hope that lightens the heavy burden of the anxious or depressed person is beautifully described in Phillips' translation of the Apostle Paul's words in Romans 8:18-26. My patients and I have often shared it.

"In my opinion whatever we may have to go through now is less than nothing compared with the magnificent future God has planned for us. The whole creation is on tiptoe to see the wonderful sight of the sons of God coming into their own.... The hope is that in the end the whole of created life will be rescued from the tyranny of change and decay, and have its share in that magnificent liberty which can only belong to the children of God.

"It is plain to anyone with eyes to see that at the present time all created life groans in a sort of universal travail. And it is plain, too, that we who have a foretaste of the Spirit are in a state of painful tension, while we wait for that redemption of our bodies which will mean that at last we have realized our full sonship in him. We are saved by this hope, but in our moments of impatience let us remember that hope always means waiting for something that we do not yet possess. But if we hope for something we cannot see, then we must settle down to wait for it in patience. The Spirit of God not only maintains this hope within us, but helps us in our present limitations."

CHAPTER 4

CAN WE LOVE AGAIN?

A lonely man sits at a bar drinking. He frequently eyes the clock to make sure he will get home late enough to go directly to bed and to sleep.

At his home, a lonely woman drops into bed. Although worn out from the responsibility of the children, she cannot sleep, and in the darkness tears roll down her cheeks.

What can one say that could generate a spark of hope in a man and a woman who have vowed "for better or for worse...till death do us part" but have found they are unable to communicate and unable to love?

That question compelled me to write about the things I have seen which produced a spark of hope in the hearts of desperate couples.

There is no need to describe the magnitude of this tragic problem. Concerned family doctors and counselors see the destructive results of broken marriages almost daily: a distraught, bitter woman; a lonely, frustrated man; a bed-wetting child; a rebellious adolescent. Every family member suffers when a marriage is on the rocks.

A college girl explained her reason for living with men

before marriage, "I want to be sure! I don't want to go through the hell my mother and father did!" This attractive girl has given herself to one man after another in search of the mysterious ingredient that was missing in her parents' marriage. In her futile search she is finding an even more grotesque caricature of real marriage than what she saw at home, and another twisted life is added to the carnage of a wrecked marriage. Broken marriages produce broken children, and the misery multiplies. If this were the whole story, the situation would be hopeless. But there is more that needs to be told. How about broken marriages that are made whole?

The word "hope" seems to have disappeared from the hearts of men and women who think the choice is to "go on living like this" or to "get a divorce." Most couples with a serious marital problem whether from unfaithfulness or a more insidious marital disease that spreads growing resentments through the years, believe that when they no longer feel love for each other the marriage is without hope.

Our counseling files prove this is a false assumption. They show that two people can not only learn to love again but they can find a more satisfying and thrilling relationship than they have ever known before. *No marriage problem is without hope as long as both partners—or, sometimes, even one partner—will hope and work.*

You recall Bill and Jan, our couple from chapter two. While I was writing that chapter, Jan and I got together again for lunch. As she brought me up to date on her happy marriage and family life, she said, "I think back and I realize it wasn't that I had so many marital problems—the problem was *me!*" I did not ask Bill about that, but I think he would say that *he* had been the problem.

Recently, a young married woman dropped in to see me. Five years ago she and her husband were separated and counseling with me. After several months of weekly visits they were reunited and moved with their children across the country.

During this visit she said, "We are still working with our problems, but one thing we know—we love each other very much." Five years ago this woman had insisted she no longer loved her husband. She said all feeling for him was gone and she could not stand to have him near. She emphatically declared that this would never change!

How did she change? It would be simple if I could give a specific formula that could heal the wounds caused by broken marriages. I have no such formula. But I have discovered how to approach some basic problems common to trouble marriages. These problems go beyond such conflict areas as money, sex, personality clashes, child training, interfering relatives, and even infidelity. These disruptions are symptoms of the real trouble rooted deep within the person.

One condition that is invariably found in an unhappy marriage is *the relationship has no meaning*.

The marriage of two people breaks down when the people break down. A marriage is meaningless when the partners have lost—or have never discovered—real meaning in life. The only lasting mending of marriages comes when a man and a woman learn the secret of living beyond themselves, when each can project himself to meet the needs of the other. This takes deep thought, confrontation, honesty, humility—all of the depth attributes that dwell inside man but which too often lie dormant under the self-life of rejection, manipulation, pride, and self-gratification.

A widely admired psychiatric view of successful marriage is contained in *The Happy Family,* by the late Dr. John Levy and his wife Ruth Munroe, a psychologist.

Each marriage is different, Dr. Levy says, but they all have one thing in common: "Every variety of marriage, if it is to be successful and enduring, has one requirement—two people shall be ready to sink themselves in the creation of a new unit bigger than either of them. The creation must be important to them. Readiness for marriage means that we can with entire honesty repeat the words: 'to love, honor, and cherish, for better or for worse, till death do us part.' Acceptance of the relationship is the big thing—not careful adjustment of money and interest and in-laws. A man and woman who are sure of their marriage, of each other, can fight openly about the other problems and work through to some sort of solution."

When there is no deep meaning in marriage, the inevitable result is loneliness. Both partners are lonely. Everyone who has come to me with marriage problems was suffering from a deep sense of loneliness.

At some time or other for all of us, there has been a period when we felt completely alone. There is a vast difference in *being* alone and in *feeling* alone. Being alone can provide a very rich and fulfilling experience, but only when we do not feel lonely and empty.

Perhaps we can best understand this in relation to one of our basic needs: communication or fellowship with another person. Milton says, "Loneliness is the first thing which God's eye named as not good." God said before he created woman that it is not good for man to be alone. Yet, in spite of that fact, many marriages produce agonizing loneliness in both partners. If all who are married could somehow grasp the depth of this basic need, we might be on the road to achieving the personal intimacy which was intended for marriage.

When this basic need for togetherness is not met in marriage, the relationship becomes sterile, boring, frustrating, and a man and woman become angry with each other because there is a bitter disapointment. This anger may be suppressed, causing resentment and hostility to smolder. Then one or the other partner may look elsewhere for someone to relate to in an intimate way. "The other woman" is often a man's attempt to fill his inner void.

CAN WE LOVE AGAIN?

A wife told me that her husband was not the type to enjoy or appreciate the deep things in life. She said he was all business and always preoccupied. Then the husband found another woman and experienced in his new relationship the closeness, acceptance, and beautiful unity he had desired with his wife. This man could have found the same intimacy with his wife—and he still can, if he wants to.

Who can deny his sincerity when he regretfully says, "I no longer love my wife; it is gone. I love someone else—I do not want an empty life any longer. I have found one who can share me as I really am. I want a divorce so I can marry the other woman."

Is it possible to help such a man open his mind to the fact that the intimacy, the completeness he feels in the new relationship is not necessarily love? If the man sincerely wanted his marriage to be a lifetime relationship and there is something inside that abhors the fact that he found intimacy with a woman other than his wife, is there hope that he may make a renewed effort to work at his marriage? If there are children involved who love both parents, will this act as a deterrent to the marital breakup? I find all of these factors involved in the spark of hope mentioned earlier.

The case of "the other man" is becoming more and more frequent in marriage counseling. At one time it was unusual for a wife to turn to another man to fill her needs, but records show there are now more women than men who are willing to leave their marriages for a new relationship.

A married woman who believed herself to be in love with another man said to me, "Do you mean to say that it is possible for me to actually love my husband again?" When I said I thought it was, she asked, "What if I never loved him in the first place? I told her that I believed it possible for her to learn to love her husband for the first time. "What if I don't *want* to love him?" I asked her if she liked the idea of a divorce, of having to admit failure in her marriage. I asked how she felt about separating the children from their father and making them adjust to a new father. Tears came as she admitted that she had not wanted this to happen—that when she married she had thought it would be for keeps and she wished it had worked out differently. So she agreed to wait and to come for counseling.

This woman and her husband came weekly for counseling. I saw them separately and discovered that each of them had personal problems that dated back to their interpersonal relationships as they were growing up. These problems affected their ability to relate to each other, and the working out of some of these problems made a reconciliation possible, but their willingness to try to meet each other's needs made the difference.

Instead of berating his wife about the other man, this husband was able to discuss him with her. She learned that she must not relate any details of her affair that would hurt him. Through listening to her description of things she had talked about with the other man and how he made her feel needed and wanted, her husband realized he had taken his wife for granted. When she told him the other man told her she was wonderful, her husband replied, "But I think you're wonderful!" "You never told me," she accused. This jolted her husband and he admitted he had not told her that since before they were married.

"How could I have been so stupid? Why did I take her so much for granted?" he asked me. "It is easy," I replied. I had been married for twenty-five years and I was trying to remember the last time I had said something like that to my husband. It had been a long time. I confessed this to my patient. He warned me, "You better go home and tell him tonight." I said I would, and I did.

Once the communication had started with these two and they continued to talk to each other, deeper understanding developed and they learned to know each other all over again. The process was beautiful to watch.

There were times of regression when both were judgmental and communication would become strained. When this happened, I suggested that they not try to discuss important issues for a while but read something relevant. I have often used Dr. Tournier's book *Guilt and Grace* for such situations. His words on the spirit of judgment proved to be very effective with this couple:

"The spirit of judgment evaporates as soon as I become conscious of my own faults and speak freely of them to my friend as he speaks to me of those which make him reproach himself.... For nothing is more contagious than confession... The spirit of judgment can thus suddenly collapse and give way to a spirit of charity, and that not by the admission which the whole logical theorem of the accusation sought to extract, but by a very different way. Precisely, by abandoning the field of logic in which accusations crossed without meeting, and by the genuine meeting of people, by a sincere revelation by each one of his real problems. The logical attitude of accusation by another and of self-defense has changed into an attitude of mind in which each one talks freely about his own difficulties and seeks to understand those of the other. And the two friends will now ask one another's forgiveness for sowing that spirit of judgment which neither wished to give up a while ago."

As each made an effort to understand and meet the other's needs, the relationship grew in warmth and maturity. Then one day they came in for a three-way conference. He had a broad grin as he told me, "I never knew marriage could be so good!" He looked at her and as her eyes met his I knew they had found each other—they loved.

During the counseling process with this couple, I was impressed with the fact that the wife progressed and gained in insight more quickly than her husband. This seemed unusual because she was the one who went astray and claimed she did not want to love her husband. Ordinarily, she would be the slow one and, because of his eagerness to keep her, he would work harder and progress faster. But she was receiving more help than he. She was a part of our weekly woman's group and had the advantage of group interaction. This realization led us to start a married couples' group. This has since become a very important adjunct in our marriage counseling. The group's role in helping mend marriages has added much to our hope for unhappy couples.

One of my most thrilling experiences in counseling came while working with a group of married couples who met each Thursday. Before a couple is invited into this group, they must have been involved in regular counseling sessions where they have become conditioned for group interaction. So many new things happen in a group. A wife sees her husband as other wives see him. She listens to what he has to say to others. One wife showed surprise in a group session as she said, "Why, my husband is smarter than I thought; he actually has some good ideas!" While it was said with a smile and intended to be facetious, a male participant sensed the underlying hostility and observed, "Maybe you're just listening, for a change!"

Another wife who had been berating her husband in the group challenged a man who objected to her outburst with: "What would you do if you were married to me?" "I'd lock you in a closet and throw away the key," he replied.

While participants are quick to sense and to react to hostility and defensiveness, they are just as sensitive to humility and listen with empathy when fellow members express their discouragement, admit their weaknesses, and reveal a willingness for help. There is a group cohesiveness that is delightful to experience. The desire to help each other is sincere, and praise is open and loud when progress is made.

After the fall and winter sessions, the couples are taken on a weekend retreat. We choose a place that is known for its restful beauty, good food, and comfortable accommodations. We reserve a comfortably furnished lounge for group dialogue, and here we see the results of the weeks of group involvement.

One couple had never taken a walk together in their twenty years of married life. More than a few eyes were misty as we saw them walk, hand in hand, in the woods.

Another couple had driven sixty miles twice a week to come for counseling and for the group session. They had dropped out for the last series but had joined us at the retreat. In one of the sessions a group member asked what had happened to them. Each told of the "miraculous" change in their marriage. They said counseling had started them on the way, the group had helped them further down the path, but it was not until they together committed themselves to God and asked his help that the important change took place and they were able to reach each other.

There was silence as they talked, and one could feel the togetherness of the group as the others were sharing the happiness of the two. There was also something about the wistful expression of some that said they hoped this could happen to them.

The experience of this couple proved again what we see so often in problems of all types. Sometimes emotional blocks must be removed before spiritual enlightenment can break through, and other times spiritual renewal must precede emotional stability. This involves such a deep distinction that I have come to believe that God alone knows which comes first, and, as his instruments, we can only proceed cautiously, expecting his Spirit to guide.

As we all work together, doctor, counselor, struggling couples, and group, we see men and women emerging as one. We see them learning in the process of sharing each other in deep intimacy and enjoying a complete and unselfish giving of oneself. This is love. When this kind of love is a part of marriage, hurting a partner causes anguish in the offender.

Unfortunately, there are times when two do not

emerge together. There are marriage situations where only one seriously struggles to make a marriage more meaningful, and it seems impossible to achieve unity no matter what that one does. This is sometimes caused by very deeply seated problems in the one who cannot relate. It may be that he is so filled with guilt that he cannot accept himself and he projects his guilt onto his mate. Such an individual needs deep therapy so that he can be helped to see what is going on inside himself. Or it may be that two are so very far apart in maturity that one cannot catch up. At such times, a decision must be made as to whether the marriage should continue.

I know one wife who feels that even though she may never achieve the completeness she yearns for in marriage there are other meaningful things in marriage she can enjoy. She admits the deep loneliness she feels at times, but she loves her husband and he needs her. She has made a mature adjustment, and she says she still has hope.

So in marriage more than in any other relationship we see two kinds of love. The first depends on and is motivated by an object outside the person loving. This love may be stimulated by beauty, personality, ability, or some other value in another person. While we cannot disregard these attractions, because they are a realistic part of love, they may subvert the deepest love by selfishly exploiting the other person. This love is inspired by something one wants for his own gratification. This love demands something in return for love, and, if thwarted or frustrated, it can turn to hate.

Pure love arises within a person who is unselfishly concerned with another's need. This love in essence is God's love within us. Can we see the Christian dimension here?

Through Christ, God revealed his love to mankind. He loved all mankind in spite of our unloveliness. He knew we needed love and acceptance, and through Christ he provided for these great needs. This kind of love is unconditional and unlimited. Despite man's unlovely nature, and acts, God loves him, and the wonderful result is that God's love created in man a response, an ability to receive love and to return it. The inimitable result is a mutually shared unselfish love.

Whether two people can achieve this love outside of unity in Christ is a difficult question. I have known couples with no apparent interest in Christianity who appear to have found a deep, unselfish love for one another. I believe, however, that a love without God at the center lacks the completeness that we all seek.

We can envision a great, devoted love extending from a woman to a man and from a man to a woman on a horizontal level, but love is truly pure and unselfish only when it flows vertically from God to man and through him to another human. This is not only a biblical teaching, but a fact of human experience.

The possibility of a man and woman achieving this complete love in marriage is a reality that inspires hope in hearts that yearn to love.

CHAPTER 5

ALCOHOLICS HOPELESS?

The words "hopeless" and "alcoholic" have long been linked to describe the excessive drinker whose dependence upon alcohol has robbed him of his freedom of choice. Whether the alcoholic is a derelict on skid row or the fashionable woman who habitually staggers out of the country club, the word "hopeless" is quickly attached by disgusted observers and friends.

What bystanders almost never know is the suffering which drives an alcoholic to his desperate state. One cannot work closely with the addicted without being touched by his misery, so I am aroused to strongly deny that any alcoholic is "hopeless."

According to surveys in this country, alcohol abuse is our largest health problem, and the third biggest killer, ranking only behind cardiovascular disease and cancer. Sixty-eight percent of all adults over the age of 21 drink. There are 10 million alcoholics in America, and probably twice that many immoderate drinkers who are potential alcoholics. It has been estimated that alcohol may be involved in up to one-third of all suicides, half of all murders, and a fourth of all other accidental deaths. The abuse of alcohol is also a major contributing factor to divorce, broken homes and child abuse, as well as a host of other problems.

In writing of alcoholic addiction in his book *The Vital Balance,* Dr. Karl Menninger deplores public apathy toward alcoholism:

"If millions of Americans were suddenly disabled with some distressing skin disease, Congress would call a special session, if necessary, to appropriate enormous sums for its study and eradication. The affliction would be visible to everyone, and the pain of its victims would arouse unusual pity. But alcohol addiction, which is also painful and disabling, can be hidden, at least for a time. The suffering it causes is not so evident; we are more than apt to laugh at its victims. And if it gets unpleasant we can always stay away from 'those people,' especially since we have the suspicion that it is a gluttonous indulgence, a chosen vice of a few ill-bred individuals. In the case of special friends and relatives, we are willing to say that it is more than a vice, it is a 'disease.'"

In the past, the alcoholic received very little attention. He was regarded as a weak individual who could quit drinking if he really wanted to. General hospitals were reluctant to give him a bed and he often ended up in jail or a state institution. Gradually the situation has changed, and today there are a variety of treatment programs to sober up the alcoholic and to discourage his drinking. He can receive medical treatment from a doctor who believes alcoholism is an organically determined condition, or go to a psychiatrist and be treated for an underlying personality disorder. He can unburden his guilt to his priest or his pastor, or he can admit he is an alcoholic, share his failures, and get on the program with Alcoholics Anonymous. There are out-patient clinics, mental health centers, alcoholism clinics, and hospitals. Private and public social agencies have open doors to the alcoholic and some industrial centers have set up alcoholic programs. If he rejects all of these extended hands, he can simply dial a number or read some of the countless books and pamphlets that tell him about himself.

Aside from the unsympathetic and uninformed attitude of the public, there are some concerned people who view alcoholics as hopeless. Why is this when there are so many sources of help available?

What if the alcoholic is not motivated to seek any help? What of the alcoholic who thinks help is O.K. for somebody else, or the one who cannot admit he is an alcoholic? What if she is one who drinks in secret and lives in dread of the day her family finds out? How about the one who cannot risk losing his way of life when he can see no better one? And there is the one who feels he is beyond hope and the only thing that keeps him alive is the fear of death, so he goes on drinking, suffering the agony of hell, blacking out, only to forget the hell and drink again.

I am thinking of all types of alcoholics as I write this chapter. I am not attempting to cover the alcoholic's problems, but to emphasize the theme of this book for the alcoholic: hope is real even for compulsive drinkers.

Members of Alcoholics Anonymous ask in a daily prayer for "the courage to change." An alcoholic once told me I could not know the kind of courage it took for an alcoholic to change because I am not one. That is true. However, I have been very close to alcoholics in counseling. No one can be involved with them without being affected by their suffering and learning something of their way of life. Also, alcoholism has deeply touched my life—my kid brother was an alcoholic.

Is this too personal to put into print? It is difficult for me to share this, for it is still a painful memory after 25 years.

Tom had a lovely wife and three children, but he was an alcoholic and he could not face it. He did not have the courage to change, he felt no hope, and he died a premature death. Tom was very close to me and I felt the tragedy deeply. He didn't have the strength to live, but he did have the "guts" to die. There are thousands of "Toms," and many others who do not die but go through a living death. Perhaps this seems melodramatic to some readers. But alcoholism seethes with emotion: struggle, shame, remorse, and striving for a change.

"Courage to change"—is this the pinpoint of hope for an alcoholic, or does hope inspire the courage to change? Is there something better if the alcoholic way of life is surrendered? Is the change worth the struggle? How can it come about?

Earlier we told the story of our first counseling patient, Bud, an alcoholic. You will recall that we knew about his failures, his torment, his depressions, and his successes—the whole person, so we could treat his real needs.

Bud had the courage to change and he had achieved sobriety, but he was an empty, frustrated man. He had not found an answer to his deep loneliness and was wondering if the struggle was worth it. Only a part of Bud's person had been treated, and not until he received treatment for his whole man did he find the vacuum filled and he could live again.

Our experience with alcoholics since Bud has convinced us that the integration of physical, mental, and spiritual treatment is essential if change is to be made.

Some specialists insist that alcoholism is roooted in a personality disorder or psychological compulsion, and there are other claims of hereditary, hormonal, metabolic, or allergic factors. But, whatever the disagreement as to causes, many are coming to agree that the medical doctor, the psychiatrist or counselor, and the pastor need to be involved in the treatment. I would add a fourth: Alcoholics Anonymous.

As an active member of AA, Bud sent many alcoholics to us, and down through the years we have kept in close contact with the AA groups. Rarely have we seen lasting success in the patient without the aid of Alcoholics Anonymous as an adjunct in therapy. Conversely, I do not know of one alcoholic who has made a satisfying adjustment in life without experiencing a spiritual meaning to life that sometimes goes beyond the AA program. I have known many alcoholics who have stopped drinking through the program and are able to stay sober, but often they exist by living in memory of the "good old days" or they replace alcohol with pills. When an alcoholic sees this as the substitute for his way of life, he questions whether it is worth it. Can the vacuum be filled with something besides pills and memories?

I think of Bill, a business executive who was referred to us by an AA group. He had been active in the program for a few months and then slipping away. This had occurred so frequently, some in his group were losing patience with him, his wife was ready to divorce him, and he was in danger of losing his job.

Bill described himself as having "hit the bottom" and considered our counseling as his last-ditch stand. He spoke in typical business terms and, in his desperation, he asked for a "blueprint," saying he would do his best to follow it.

We pointed out to Bill that the "blueprint" would involve his whole person—physical, mental, and spiritual. At first Bill resisted the idea of "bringing religion" into the treatment, and no pressure was put on him. When he said he did not believe in God, he was told that was his right and we would treat him in the other two areas. After three conferences, Bill brought up the topic of religion, confessing that he really wasn't an atheist and adding, "Maybe a peek at the religious side wouldn't hurt—but I'm not promising to buy it."

The weeks that followed were not easy, but Bill was determined to succeed. As hours became days and days became weeks, he refused liquor, his courage grew stronger, and hope for sobriety became a reality. After two months of concentrated treatment which included spiritual therapy, Bill had a very real spiritual experience which involved complete confession and commitment to God.

During one of our sessions we had discussed where God fit into his life. The time stretched into a two-hour conference as he asked deep questions about God, Jesus Christ, guilt, forgiveness, and how it all affected him. He seemed depressed when he left the office and I was concerned. He told me the next morning what had happened when he left the clinic.

As he drove down the highway toward his home, he thought about our session and he began to doubt that God would really help him. He thought, "This faith stuff is not for me. Maybe some guy who hasn't led a rotten life could be accepted, but it's not for me."

His hands started trembling and an uncontrollable urge to drink came over him. He pushed on the accelerator and raced toward the nearest bar. Then a thought pushed its way into his racing mind: "What if God would be willing to forgive me and I'd mess it all up by drinking again?" He pulled over to the side of the road and put his head down on the steering wheel and prayed. He did not remember ever praying before in his life. A peaceful calm came over him. He looked at his hands as he drove home and they were not shaking. He felt quiet inside. When he reached home, his wife looked at him and said, "Something has happened to you, Bill. You're different. I have never seen you look like this."

From that day on there was a difference in Bill's progress. His life had meaning. He started building his life on a foundation that was steady and, in time, his family joined a church, his situation at his office stabilized, and he became a respected and sought-after leader in his AA group.

Were all of Bill's problems solved? Was life peaceful and stable thereafter? How unrealistic! Bill's process of getting well in all three areas of his life had only started. He has no promise (not even from God!) that he will not suffer or face serious problems. The difference is that he does not feel empty, hopeless, or alone. And he isn't. He knows where he stands with God—accepted. He has found his true identity.

Is Bill's an isolated case? Many other alcoholics come to mind as I examine my files. There are men and women and a few young people, but some of them stand out in my memory above others.

There was Jack; the day our friend Bud was to leave for Florida, he missed his plane so he could talk to Jack and refer him to us.

Jack, a beauty shop owner, was in his late twenties. He had started drinking heavily when in his teens. He married a beautician who excelled in her field and Jack rode along on her ability. He managed the shop, but her skill and popularity brought success. Jack felt insecure and inferior and he used alcohol as an escape. They quarreled bitterly and frequently, and when he was referred for counseling she had started divorce proceedings.

Jack's treatment involved marriage counseling as well as treatment for his alcoholism. Because he had seen what had happened in Bud's life, he did not resist spiritual help. After he had come to understand man's relation to God, he carried a small black book with Scripture passages jotted down.

One of his most difficult problems involved fussy women customers. Whenever he became tense in the shop, he would go to the back room and read the Scripture verses and "talk to God." He described his talks as going something like this: "Look, God, you know me, how I am; I don't think you can change Mrs. __________, but you'd better take away this pressure or I'm going to walk out and you know where I'll go. These verses here—if they're from you to me—make them work fast." To some theologians such words might be faulty doctrine if not sacrilege, but Jack's method worked.

He described his experiences as "just like someone else

was there in that little back room with me, and I settled down inside."

One day Jack said he counted fifteen times he went to the back room.

It was after these back room experiences that Jack was able to accept the part of spiritual therapy which had been difficult for him—the death of Christ on the cross for Jack's sins. Today Jack has not had a drink in 22 years; he has two children, is happily married, and he recognizes the shop would not run without his management.

Are these two stories saying that an alcoholic's problems will be solved if he commits his life to God? We cannot claim such a cut-and-dried answer for so complex a problem. What does the climb from rock bottom to a life filled with meaning involve for the alcoholic?

There is always a first step. That step for many is the courage to leave their way of life. In spite of the dreadful pain and fear within the alcoholic, he feels a certain amount of security so long as he can drown his thoughts in alcohol. Even though he may know this escape is driving him toward destruction, he dreads to let go. He cannot be sure of the alternative. If he can find the courage to change, or if he, through hope, can believe there is something better, he can take the all-important first step.

When that step is taken, a process is set in motion. Good rapport and faith and trust in the doctor and counselor is essential. If he can accept the fact that at least one person believes in him, he can ride along on the counselor's faith when he cannot trust himself.

I tell my alcoholics to call me any hour of the day or night if they feel they are headed for that first drink. Once I received a call in the middle of the night. One of my alcoholics was across country in another city and there were several hours difference in the time. After he apologized for waking me, he told me he had been struggling all evening to keep out of a bar but he had lost the battle. He was inside and he knew he was going to drink. I asked him why he called me. His voice trembled as he said he didn't know but he knew he couldn't make it on his own. I asked him where the phone was situated and he said it was a few yards from the bar. When I asked if he could see the front door from where he was, he said he could. I told him to keep his eyes on the door as he hung up and do it.

When this man returned home he described the experience as "sheer will power over my feet. My whole body felt dead but my eyes on the door brought me throught it." He also told me of the strange and wonderful power he felt after he was in his car driving to his hotel. He thought, "It's that 'babe' back there—I'll bet she's praying for me."

The "babe" was, and I told him I did not care what he called me so long as he called when he needed help.

So the alcoholic is dependent, and our experience convinces us that he must be allowed to exercise dependence when necessary. However, there needs to be an underlying firmness by the counselor so the alcoholic learns a sense of responsibility.

The daily, weekly, or bi-weekly visits to a counselor can become a drag, but if the alcoholic trusts the judgment of the one who is helping and he accepts his responsibility to be there, he will make the effort.

Regular attendance at AA meetings is not so difficult after the ice is broken and the alcoholic is convinced of the necessity of following the AA steps. Sometimes other responsibilities crowd in and he must be reminded that his therapy must come first.

Counseling sessions which include husbands or wives of alcoholics can add stress, but this is a vital part of the treatment program as the mate can prevent rehabilitation. Many times the partner needs as much therapy as the alcoholic.

Admission that they cannot drink seems very difficult for some alcoholics. Some use the ulcer excuse; they would rather admit to an ulcer than to alcoholism. Then there is the alcoholic who will hold one drink in his hand all evening at the cocktail party and torture himself with the smell of alcohol under his nose rather than tell the host he cannot drink.

So the struggle goes on every hour, every day, week after week, month after month. Should we wonder when he asks, "Is it worth it?" It is important at times like this for him to talk to someone further along in the struggle. I can remember Bud's response when he was asked that question:

"What is your choice, brother?" he asked bluntly.

There was no answer. To go back to the alcoholic way of life was unthinkable, so the courage to change was strengthened.

So while commitment to God is not the complete answer, our experience with alcoholics has shown that a spiritual relationship to God produces power that exceeds human resolution, and the burden of change grows lighter as new life fills the vacuum with meaning.

When the power of God is sustaining the alcoholic, it is as though he has guardian angels around him. We see this often, and there is one experience that our staff will never forget.

One evening I was in conference and suddenly I felt a strange concern for an alcoholic patient. I tried to dismiss the distraction, but the concern grew stronger and stronger. I tried to tell myself that Matt was coming along all right and there was no need for concern. But the feeling would not leave and I finally excused myself. Fortunately, I was not in conference with a seriously disturbed patient. I asked our receptionist to contact Matt or his wife and see if everything was all right.

At the end of my conference I discovered that Matt's wife did not know where he was. He had been gone all day and not come home. After running down all other possibilities, I called one of Matt's friends and obtained the name of the hotel where Matt went when he was drinking.

By this time I was certain Matt was in trouble. I called

the police and reported that I had reason to believe this patient was in danger. The police went to the hotel and as they approached his room they could smell gas. They broke down the door and carried Matt out in time to save his life. Matt had meant business. In a moment of weakness he had taken a drink and his remorse was so strong he could not stand himself. He went to his room, methodically sealed all the cracks with newspapers, and turned on a gas jet.

I do not make a claim to possess ESP or any psychic powers—to me there is only one answer: the power of God in divine intervention.

Anyone who works with alcoholics knows there will be some who will not make it. There was the attractive woman who left my office rejecting the treatment of the whole person. Alnd she wanted nothing to do with AA—she could do it herself.

A week later fire engines raced past my window. That alcoholic burned to death in her home that day; there was an empty bottle and cigarette butts beside her. She could not do it herself. There have been many others.

The alcoholic knows even better than the counselor that defeat is near. He knows it will claim some, but he does not want to be defeated so he may have the courage to change. But he cannot do it alone. If he can believe he can't do it alone, he need not agonize alone. There are many sources of help available, but nearer than all of these human hands is the extended hand of God—all the alcoholic needs to do is reach out and grasp it.

CHAPTER 6

THE SEARCHING GENERATION

As I have worked with young people for more than twenty-five years, there is one word that describes them to me. That word is *search.* Young people are searching inward to find who they are, searching outward to determine their place in life and searching for another to satisfy the longing for intimacy and sense of belonging. They are looking for a meaning to life. They seek love, self-worth and success.

During the late 1940's I was associated with Young Life, a national organization that works with high school young people. Its purpose is to introduce them to Christianity in a way that is relevant to them. While my primary responsibility was editing the *Young Life* magazine, I had considerable contact with teen-agers. They taught me much. Their honest, frank approach to life was refreshing. They were searching for answers, and they wanted answers not adages.

While the basic needs of young people are the same today as they were forty years ago, the world is vastly different, and if we are to help them find answers we must first understand their world.

The adult world was astonished at the reactions when Beatle, John Lennon was shot and killed. "It was like the death of a president" seemed to describe the feelings of many who a decade ago were among the teenagers who idolized and mobbed the Beatles.

Many adults had thought the Beatlemania was over, then suddenly, the TV and news media gave upfront time and space to John Lennon, who had long since given over his popularity to other rock stars.

This phenomenon has a message that adults need to hear. The Beatles sang and talked of the deep concerns of young people. Sure there were sex, rebellion, drugs and all of the negatives that worried adults but there were also songs that told of freedom, lonely people, ecology, war and peace, nuclear power and fear of failure.

The explosive reactions to John Lennon's death prove that the contemporary crowd is still searching.

In recent years I have noticed this searching becoming more intense. Some seem almost desperate in their need for love and self-worth and they are going beyond conventional boundaries to find success and meaning to life. When their search does not bring satisfying results in reality, many continue to turn to alcohol, sex and drugs hoping to find answers in a world of fantasy. Young people want answers to the same basic problems as their predecessors but their hang-ups are different because their world is different.

To us adults, that different world is intolerable. For example, many of us see the experimental living together as a radical departure from all we consider sacred in family life and we grit our teeth to refrain from judgmental condemnation.

Do we stop to consider that these outward manifestations are only superficial symptoms of real needs? Can we see that the real conflicts are inward and are imbedded in such important issues as lack of acceptance, need for love and fear of failure?

Can these young people find meaning to life when all around them they see adults searching for the same meaning and not finding it?

THE SEARCHING GENERATION

When I talk to my young friends about hope, they give me a look that says "Show me!" Some who cannot face me stand at the window looking out, and their stance is itself a deep cry of "Show me." When the mask of "I couldn't care less" is dropped from the face of a young person and I see the depth of his inner unrest, I become both angry and sad. Angry because of what our world has done to push them into this turmoil, and sad because there are so very many of them and it will take such a long struggle for them to emerge from their confusion.

The question is, Will they emerge? Is there help for mainliners, pot smokers, unhappy misfits, and the kids who are simply confused? And do they really want help?

To answer the second question first, I have never met a disturbed young person, who, when he is finally able to relate, will not admit he needs help. It is a short step from this admission to a genuine desire, and when this is coupled with the assurance that there is hope he will usually keep coming for help.

A nineteen-year-old girl rode her bike twenty miles each way every Saturday for her appointment. She does not want her parents to know she is coming for help. "They would never understand—they have no idea how messed up I am," she confided. Another girl drove 120 miles a week for her session. She worked and earned a modest salary, and was the only patient I had who paid several weeks in advance. "I don't want to take a chance on spending my money for something else," she explained.

My experience with these young people has convinced me that they want help, and they are giving us all kinds of signs. These signs may not always be easy to understand. Their calls for help may be hidden behind running away, sexual promiscuity, drug abuse, and attempted suicide. They may not recognize that they are calling out for help and that the call is coming from deep inside of them.

Where do they expect to receive help? Most of them are not looking to the adult generation. They are convinced that adults are from another world. Their parents, of all people, would not understand, and they have their own hang-ups and miseries. Because acceptance by peers is of prime importance to youth, they go to their mixed-up friends for help and advice...and the blind lead the blind.

We adults need to ask ourselves: Are we willing to listen? Has it occurred to us that we might learn something from our young people?

Could the adult be having difficulty with his adolescent because he himself has unresolved adolescent conflicts? Is today's adult adolescently competitive? Are adults insecure and frightened by life in the twentieth century? Is there really a generation gap, after all? Might the adult and the adolescent help each other?

I would not have the courage to suggest the last possibility if I had not seen results in the area of adult-adolescent involvement.

In past years, more than a dozen girls have lived as a part of our family in our home—some of them staying for as long as a year or two. We rarely had more than one at a time and each one seemed very special to us. While their problems varied, they all had at least two common needs: they lacked a sense of self-worth and a feeling of being accepted and loved. My evaluations and conclusions drawn from living with these girls would fill another book, but a few illustrations here will convey my optimism.

There was a quiet, sweet, seventeen-year-old with a conservative, genteel home background. She had no serious problems as she was growing up. Then when she went to high school things began to happen. She became involved with the wrong crowd, and when she was brought to the clinic her parents could no longer control her activities. She had become resentful and angry and was filled with guilt. Some of the guilt was false but some very real. This girl was convinced that her only route was to continue in her present pattern. She thought "decent" people would not want her.

There was another girl with us from a foreign country.

Her boy friend had sent for her and then decided not to marry her. She was stranded.

One nineteen-year-old was so bottled up with fear she had difficulty speaking when she first came to us.

Young, unwed mothers have been a part of our foster family. Some came before their babies arrived, some afterward.

One of the most difficult and most needy of all our girls came through a call from the juvenile officer at the county jail. She told me, "There's a girl down here who will be sent to the school for girls tomorrow unless we find a home for her."

I knew the "school for girls." Hardened, unscrupulous girls lived there, some because of serious offenses.

"Is she a delinquent? What has she done?" I asked.

"She has never been booked for serious trouble, but she cut her wrists and we just don't have anywhere else to send her."

I went to the jail and found a scared, seventeen-year-old girl. She looked more boy than girl. An overgrown pixie haircut made it difficult to see her eyes. She looked at the floor and picked at a ragged edge of her jeans as she answered my questions.

She said she didn't know whether it would be possible for me to trust her or not. She couldn't trust herself. She said she couldn't promise me anything because she didn't know herself what she would do next.

I decided this was either the most honest girl I had ever met or the best con artist. I later discovered she was both. I told her I would have to discuss it at home and I would let her know the first thing the following day. She looked up at me then and I shall never forget that look. All of the tough facade was gone and her eyes were big with fright as she said, "I really would like to live with you, but I won't blame you one bit if you say no."

It was a serious decision for us to make, for two reasons. Since this would probably be our daughter Joan's last year at home, perhaps we should not have anyone else in the home; and in two weeks we were to leave for a much-needed vacation.

After I had presented the situation to my husband and daughter, it was Joan who decided for us. She said, "We just can't let her go out to *that* place, and, besides, I'd get pretty bored around here all alone." I considered Joan a wise girl—and one who knew her mother very well.

I brought Les home with me the next day, explaining that in two weeks we would be going away on vacation and it would be necessary then for her to stay with someone else for several weeks. I promised her it would be a "good" place.

Les had been shifted from one foster home to another since she was eight when her mother died. Ours was the ninth home she had lived in. She said she was looking for the right place and something to take away the scared feeling she always had.

The adjustment for Les was difficult, but she said she felt safe in our home. One night after she had been with us about a week, my husband was out of town and I woke up in the middle of the night with the strange feeling that someone was in the room. It was dark. I could not see but I felt a presence. I turned over and Les's scared voice said, "It's just me, Mrs. G." I turned on the light, and Les was sitting on the floor beside my bed, shivering. It was an incongruous sight to see the seemingly self-sufficient, tough girl hunched over and shaking with fear. She said she had had a nightmare—a horrible one that she often had, and she thought she'd feel safe if she could just sit near me the rest of the night. We went to her room where she drank some warm milk and I sat on the edge of her bed much as I had done years before when my small children had awakened from a bad dream. She soon fell asleep.

We feared that Les's leaving our home even temporarily would be very difficult for her, but she had covered up beautifully. She met her new house parents and said she would enjoy being with them. Then the evening came for the move, and while the couple came in the front door Les suddenly vanished out the back door. A two-hour search brought no results, and our friends went home without her. I watched out the window and waited. I prayed Les would come back. I could not frighten her by calling in the police. The strumming of Joan's guitar in the family room annoyed me: here I was, worrying about Les, and Joan was playing music.

Some time later I saw Les coming across the field next to our house. Her head was down as her long strides brought her to the back door. I opened the door but she ignored my outstretched hand and slumped into a kitchen chair. She would not talk, so I sat at the table silently waiting. Then she took a razor blade from her pocket and started to slide it across her wrists. I watched without moving. She toyed with it for a while, then blurted out angrily, "You don't think I'll do it, do you?"

"I know you can, Les, for you have done it before."

Hearing Les's voice, Joan came into the kitchen with her guitar in hand. If she saw the razor blade she ignored it.

"Les, I wrote a song while you were gone—want to hear it?"

Les was surprised. She put the razor down and answered, "Yeah."

I left and listened from the other room. The song Joan had written spoke of Les's past life and the fear which made her run from everything and everybody. But it also challenged her to be patient enough in her search to stop and look for the answer that might be behind the next door.

"You wrote that for me? Well, I'll be...I never did have anyone write a song about me. How about that!"

The next day Les went to her temporary home.

Les stayed with us for a year. She went to school, worked at odd jobs, reacted, rebelled, hated school, at times threatened me with her fists, put a hole in her bedroom door, but at the same time was growing up. She knew we loved her.

When Les became eighteen something happened to her. While we could understand it, it was a deep disappointment. She decided she no longer needed help—no one was to tell her what to do. We could no longer structure her in even the slightest regulations.

We told our girls that if the time came when they would not live within our family structure they can no longer be in the family, and the day came when I had to give Les an ultimatum. She was either to agree to live within the structure or she would have to go.

It was a cold, snowy, winter night. She stormed out of the back door wearing only a thin jacket and stopped in the middle of the field. She knew I could see her and she was waiting for me to call her back. I could not.

Les went away then and I did not see her again until three months later when she showed up one night at my office. She was high on drugs and wanted to come back to our home to live. I wanted to bundle her in my car and take her home, but I knew I could not handle her in our home while she was on drugs. I offered to find a place where she could be helped, but she yelled some four-letter words at me and stamped out of the clinic.

Somehow I believed we would see Les again though we lost all track of her. Doubtless we made mistakes with Les, but our experience convinced me that adults and adolescents can relate positively to each other.

This chapter was finished and all ready for the publisher when I received a phone call from Les. Her familiar deep voice said, "Hi, Mrs. G., know who this is?"

She said she had been driving past the house all evening trying to get up courage to come in. Finally she went to a telephone booth and called. I asked her to come right over.

I opened the door and stared at the lovely girl in the

doorway. Her hair that had been short and shaggy now fell softly to her shoulders. The scared, bitter look was gone. She smiled at my astonishment.

We talked for hours. I learned that she had slammed out of the clinic into one dead-end after another, and had "traveled" on drugs and alcohol. Then a former school teacher "tricked" her into a hospital for a drug cure. There she started thinking.

She said she remembered many of the things we had told her—especially about God and Jesus Christ. After long months in the hospital she was taken to live with a Christian woman who continued to help her in her spiritual growth. She said she wanted to be sure first that she was not going to regress into her old habits.

As I watched this new person before me, perhaps I should have wondered where I had failed with her but I didn't. It may have been because I had punished myself many times with those thoughts since she went away, but I think, rather, it was because I have learned that I am only a link in a chain of human helpers. And our home was an important link for Les when she needed it.

Les was working part time with the police department, helping other girls and going to school. As she put it, "It takes a con to handle a con. Those kids are up against something when they try to con me." Les came to our home regularly then and was a real friend to the newest foster member of our family.

So they came and went and each time one left there was a sense of loss in our home. We remember these girls as we do our own two children. There were times they tested us and other times when they retreated within themselves and we could not get through. There were the episodes of rebellion, as when Jerry insolently blew tobacco smoke in my face, or Sonny came to her conferences with a transistor radio turned up high. Later it was Sonny who insisted that the music in the house be turned down when my car pulled into the drive.

CAN I HOPE AGAIN?

From our experience, we believe the way to extend help significantly is for adults to accept the possibility that the generation gap is only what we allow it to be. We believe that it is possible for two generations to work together in their search for answers.

I could not name all of the adults who played a part in Les's rehabilitation. There was the concerned juvenile officer who did not want to see her go to a correctional school. There were the judge, policemen, and others representing law and order who backed me when I took her home. There was a high school principal and teachers, the hospital personnel director who gave her a job, and Young Life staffers who made room for her at a Colorado ranch when they were already overcrowded.

After Les left us, there continued to be helpful adults along the way: the teacher who would not give up until she was in a hospital for treatment for drug addiction, another teacher who gave her a home when she was released from the hospital, and others. You may have noticed the "help" group that was missing were Les's own peers! Aside from a couple of friends she made who also were messed up, and my daughter and her friends, Les was an "outsider" to her peers who might have helped her.

Unfortunately, for every adult who helped, there was at least one who hindered. Some of them could not give because of their own problems, and others rejected Les because they have not realized what is happening in the young generation.

We started with the question of hope for young people. I asked Les for some answers to that question. Her first reaction was negative; she was afraid to express her opinions for anything that might appear in print. We talked about it, and soon her feelings about adults came to the surface. Her positive opinions revealed her appreciation for those who had helped; her negative reactions, surging from unforgotten rejections, hurts, and fears, were bitter, and I saw again the rejected child I had brought into our home six years before.

Les repeatedly came back to one statement: "You just aren't one of them. No matter how you change, you're still an outsider." Though she was primarily describing her life in foster homes, she said she felt that way about most adults.

"They won't let you forget you have been a mixed-up kid. I still run into this with both Christian and non-Christian adults. They'll say you're great and you've made such wonderful progress, and you get to thinking you maybe have it made with them—and then if you don't agree with their ideas or don't dress or behave just like they think you should, you can see in their eyes and the shake of their heads they're thinking: 'She was a drug addict, you know.'"

So, the searching continues. Perhaps young people are looking for true meaning to life because we have not shown it to them. They are looking for acceptance; do we accept them? They are looking for success; do they see us as successful? They are looking for love; do we love them? They are trying to find God; do they see him in us? Are we also searching?

CHAPTER 7

THE HEALING OF FAMILIES

Many individuals in our modern society need hope desperately. What about the families of these distressed people...does one member's disorientation infect the family, or does family conflict produce disturbances in the individual? Are both true?

Relatively little research has been completed on the influence of the family on individual personality, but psychiatry is beginning to look in this direction and many therapists have begun family treatment programs.

Our group has not researched the effect of the family on the individual, or vice versa, but we have evaluated the family pattern when we have taken an individual into therapy. Often this has led to conferences with family members. This seemed the only complete and effective method of treating an individual. I have no doubt that one disturbed family member can affect the others similarly to the spreading of a contagious disease.

Most of the emphasis in child training has been placed on the mother's influence, but experience has taught us that mental health is much more involved than that. We hear much about the depriving, rejecting, overprotecting, or seductive mother, but though the mother certainly plays a vital role in the development of the child there are other factors of significant importance. How about the father's relationship with the mother? How does the value system of each parent affect the family? A host of other influences are found in the disturbed person, whether that person is a child or adult.

A disturbed personality fosters confusion throughout the family. The person who is emotionally ill or suffering from inner conflicts does not know why he acts and feels as he does. Often, a distraught patient has said to me, "I feel all mixed up... I don't know why I do the things I do." The problem is further complicated by the way in which surface symptoms and verbalization obscure basic underlying problems. It is no wonder that the rest of the family lose their sense of balance and become irrational in their efforts to cope. This irrational interaction between family members is termed "confusion" in this chapter.

When our friend, Bud, the alcoholic, was having serious problems, he and his wife realized the destructive effects upon the children. When he began to make progress in straightening out his life, his relationship to his children was dramatically affected. The same was true in each case we have discussed in this book.

The couple who walked off hand-in-hand at our weekend retreat for their first walk together were just beginning to communicate. They continued in family therapy for some time before they could function together in a healthy marriage.

Sometimes couples in conflict are not convinced they need help until they realize how seriously their disturbance is affecting their children. Often the easier way out is taken: the disturbed individual is sent to a hospital or a correctional school, and the family problem remains untouched. As we have seen emotional confusion infecting whole families—and concentrated family therapy producing positive results—we are convinced that the treatment of the whole person must extend to the treatment of the entire family.

THE HEALING OF FAMILIES

One morning I received a frantic call from the mother of seven-year-old Mike. Because of Mike's school phobia I had been involved in family counseling with Mike, his parents, his brother, and his sisters. Mike's mother was calling from the school. "Mike is out in the station wagon. He just won't come in. I've tried everything you've suggested. Now he has found a pair of sharp pliers in the car and is pinching his neck. He is bleeding." She said the school principal had tried to help but Mike would not budge.

I talked to the principal, who had also been involved with us in Mike's problem. In a more objective manner, she described the situation.

When Mike had refused to leave the car, his mother had sought help from the principal. It was a cold, snowy morning and Mike had taken off his shoes and socks in his attempt to control the situation. When they threatened to carry him, he grabbed the pliers and clamped them on his neck.

In past months of counseling, progress had been made in the family situation and Mike's mother had learned to cover up her concern when Mike tried to get control by his bizarre methods, but the sight of blood on Mike's neck terrified her and Mike had regained control of the situation.

I saw this episode as a desperate test Mike was giving his mother and, in turn, all of us. I told the principal that Mike would lose months of progress if he won this battle, and he was to go into the school no matter what he did.

"Even in bare feet in the snow?"

"Even in his bare feet!"

The two women literally dragged Mike from the car and pulled him barefooted through the snow, pliers still hanging on his neck. At the door, his mother quickly left him.

As soon as Mike was in the principal's office, he stopped crying, allowed her to dry his feet, put on his shoes and stockings, and apply a bandaid to his throat. Then she called me and put Mike on the phone.

I asked him what was wrong.

"I wanted *you* to bring me. I'm not scared when you bring me." He was still trying to control his sobs.

"But I told you I would not be bringing you anymore, remember?"

"Yeah, but I still wanted you to."

"Mike, can we talk about this when I see you tomorrow?"

"I want to see you today."

"Our time is tomorrow, Mike."

"They made me walk in my bare feet in the snow."

"Why was that?"

After a long silence he admitted, "I wouldn't put my shoes on."

"Then, who made you walk barefooted?"

"I guess I did..."

We talked for a few minutes and Mike agreed to wait for his regular appointment to see me. That desperate effort to control was Mike's last. He made a good adjustment in school and his family interaction was greatly improved.

My purpose is not to examine the reasons for Mike's school phobia. I want to illustrate how his problem—which originated in the family—affected every member. And not until all family members and related individuals were involved in counseling was significant progress made.

Mike was brought to me initially because he refused to go to school. Before he came to us, he had been coaxed, threatened, punished, loved, given extra attention, and ignored. Some of these methods worked temporarily, but Mike would slip right back to his old pattern of playing sick, sobbing uncontrollably, or just refusing to go to school. Because of what seemed to be a realistic fear, his parents took him out of a private school and enrolled him in public school. When this failed, Mike was brought to us.

Before long, it was obvious that Mike's problem was centered in family personality difficulties and conflicts. Mike was not afraid to go to school—he was afraid to leave his home. One by one, family members were brought into counseling. Perhaps we were fortunate that all concerned were desperate by the time we entered the picture so the way was cleared for complete cooperation. Therapy involved family conferences and consultations with Mike's teacher and the school principal. Visits were made at the school and in the home. I had to be available for phone calls and early-morning trips to school with Mike.

Mike subjected me to many tests. One of the most difficult was the day he brought his hamster to my office. I feel about hamsters the way many women feel about mice. As we were talking, he let the animal out of its box and it crawled around on the carpet. Mike watched gleefully as the furry thing crawled over to me and slipped up over my instep. My whole being revolted, but outwardly I appeared to ignore it. When I did not react as Mike had expected, he grinned and picked up his pet and put it back in the box.

Surviving Mike's little tests was a part of the process of acceptance that later led toward progress in the family problem. The team-work we discussed in chapter two made success eventually possible: father, mother, brother, sisters, teachers, principal, priest, and counselor working together with Mike brought lasting results.

In recent years the importance of the individual's learning to solve his own problems has almost become fanaticism with some psychiatrists. I believe the result for many adolescents has been a "hate your parents" compulsion.

Personal responsibility is essential if one is to gain maturity. In the effort to assure it, many have ignored the family unit as the ideal place to develop healthy individuality.

Perhaps it is not necessary here to emphasize the unique role of the family, and yet, with society's concepts and values changing so rapidly, it might be well to remind ourselves of the consequences of family disruption. Must family unity be destroyed by an emotional illness, before we are aware of its importance?

It is notable that no society has ever succeeded in eliminating the family. The Russian Communists tried to radically alter the family by lax regulations of divorce and marriage, doing away with family inheritance, and other measures. But so many stresses developed that the policies were reversed. The kibbutzim of Israel which at first provided specialized agencies for child care and rearing outside the family unit were revised toward a more traditional family life.

Some leaders in the social sciences are convinced that many of today's social ills stem from disruption of the family unit and they are working toward restoring stability.

American parents voiced their concern over family breakdown in response to a nationwide telecast. Evangelist Billy Graham reported that several million viewers had written to him about current problems, and though they were concerned about youth reactions, immorality, alcoholism, and economic problems, family problems were at the top of the list.

From our experience in working with families, we are hopeful because we have seen results. Sometimes these results have come surprisingly quickly as family members became aware of their part in the conflicts. Basically, families want to be together. I have seen this time after time as I have worked with disturbed people. Perhaps surprisingly, this is particularly true of children and adolescents.

I recall a situation of several years ago. A woman came in to talk about her seven-year-old girl who had been put in an orphanage five years earlier and now was coming back with her mother. I assumed the mother wanted help in the child's adjustment to home life, but as the woman talked I realized the woman did not want her child. Her whole life was wrapped up with her new husband, and the child would be in the way of her having a good time.

"The trouble is," she explained, "the kid wants to live with us. It's silly. She has friends at the orphanage. It's a good place. I intend to return her."

She wanted my help in persuading the child to stay where she was. As I watched the cold woman, I felt her child might well be better off in the orphanage. I asked to see the girl.

She was tiny and shy. She sat in the chair like a little lady, her hands folded in her lap. I asked how she liked the orphanage. She said she liked it fine but now she was old enough to live at home. She wanted to help her mother; she could sweep, dust, do dishes, and even cook a little. "Besides," she added, "I want to live in *my* home with *my* mother. I belong there. Will you tell my mother I should live at home—please? She thinks I'll miss the other kids."

I talked to the woman again. I asked how her husband felt about the child. She said he liked her. He had never had any of his own and wanted to keep her. There was disgust in her voice. I suggested that he come in to see me.

As the woman left, I doubted she would give her husband my message. I never saw any of them again. I have often regretted not taking the child home with me. But that would not have been *her* home—she wanted her *real* mother, her *real* home.

Without exception, every teen-age girl who lived with us revealed the same yearning for her own home and her own parents. Though they wished their parents were different, they often made excuses for them. Though they rebelled against them and said nasty things about them, they still wanted their own homes and parents. Unfortunately, some of them never found what they wanted.

Most parents also want family unity. Occasionally we meet a cold parent like the little orphan's mother, but this is the exception. How often I have heard a mother's sobs of guilt when she speaks of the effects the home disturbance is having on the children. The helplessness that a mother and a father feel when the whole family is caught up in their problems adds to their own confusion, and a chain reaction is set into motion that is difficult to break. Regardless of whether the individual or the family is the primary cause of emotional breakdown, all members are affected and mass confusion is the result.

One of the first goals I try to establish when beginning family counseling is to emphasize the importance of the basic needs of family members. When parents are too busy or blind to the simple things that make up our childrens' needs, they try to buy satisfaction with things—and both parents and children lose out.

I am writing this chapter on the small island of Bonaire in the Dutch Antilles, and I wondered when I came how the island might inspire me in writing about the family. The island is arid and sparsely vegetated, and there are few inhabitants. But I have had new and delightful experiences as I discovered little things that are hidden away out of sight.

As I now watch a tiny, long-legged bird run along the beach beside the water, he seems crazy. He runs fast for a few steps, jerks his head out, stops, then repeats the performance. If I had not watched this same little bird—or his brother—the day before with binoculars, he would seem strange indeed. I had been focusing the lens on some beautiful flamingos the day before when I noticed the little bird running. The binoculars disclosed that he was running into a swarm of tiny gnats. He would snap one, eat it, then charge into the swarm again. I forgot the flamingos in fascination at the little bird's performance.

Then I discovered varieties of marine life hiding in shells and tiny lizards sneaking up outdoor tables after diners had left. I watched delightedly as a tiny fellow slipped up on my writing table and shot out his long, red tongue dozens of times until he had methodically covered a ring left by a coffee cup.

THE HEALING OF FAMILIES

The most awesome discovery was made while visiting the underwater home of sea inhabitants. I had been in glass-bottomed boats, but never donned a mask and fins and watched the fantastic kingdom deep beneath the waves. It was easy to forget the problem-world above when face to face with placid, beautiful fish! So I ventured into the lovely world of little things—and I found my analogy for the family.

We need to "discover" each other. We need to look beyond surface appearances, take time to observe and understand, creatively interact with others and see what they are really like. How little we know about our families! We may well be delightfully surprised when we discover how little it takes of *us* to satisfy the needs we are trying to fill with *things.*

Ask any child what he remembers about his early childhood. His answers will include seemingly little events that involve *people.* When I asked my daughter what she remembered most about her childhood, she told of the time she and her daddy had walked to the drug store. My son laughingly recalled: "The time Dad tripped over the coffee table." This came from children who had seen much of the United States and Europe.

As I have watched family life change in the process of therapy, it is always rewarding to hear fathers admit that spending a little time listening to their children was not so bad after all. Sometimes they are surprised to discover abilities and ideas that they did not dream existed in their children.

When a family is in conference together, the parents often have difficulty listening to what the children have to say. They are so accustomed to telling their children what to do that they lack the patience to listen.

Recently a fifteen-year-old girl returned home after a month's disappearance. She asked to come home, and her parents traveled to another state to get her. In my office she said her parents listened to what she had to say for the first time on the ride back.

Another girl who returned home after being separated from her parents while all were involved in therapy tells how her father has changed. Before, he had "always exploded the minute I opened my mouth"; now he "starts to react, stops himself, grumbles an apology, and listens." She is responding and has decided her dad "isn't such a bad guy after all."

A mother of ten, five of them her own, five the children from her husband's former marriage, describes the reaction when she started listening to the children, speaking in low, quiet tones, touching a child kindly as she spoke or listened. At first her ten-year-old boy looked at his sister and asked in a worried tone, "What's with *her?*" But after the mother admitted to them that she had been making mistakes and wanted to do a better job, she not only found cooperation but two self-appointed sergeants who kept the smaller ones in line.

When goals are understood, parents often choose their own methods for establishing family communications. In one family a certain time is designated when children talk and parents listen. The mother said she had no idea it would be so difficult to listen without interrupting. She said she realized she had been rude to her children. "They have learned their lack of respect from us!" she admitted.

As communication lines are opened and family members come to know each other, resentment and hostility dissolve even though a basic problem may not be resolved.

One woman told me, "It is tragic how we can know the right things to do and yet be unable emotionally to do them." This woman had read the best books on child raising, was active in PTA, atended lectures, and was involved in duscussion groups, but emotionally she could not cope with her family. It took a near tragedy with one of her teen-agers to induce her to put her knowledge into action.

THE HEALING OF FAMILIES

We hear much about self-insight—that the most important goal for an emotionally ill person is to gain understanding of himself. I believe this is important, but my experience with people has convinced me that insight alone is futile and often makes the sick one more frustrated and depressed. Unless goal-directed action can be fused with the insight, progress is frozen.

We have watched families progress from confusion and almost total lack of communication to meaningful interchange and unity in action. This does not necessarily result in uniformity of thought and opinions, of course. I have never known one patient to make progress and fail to affect others by his change. Nowhere is this more noticeable than in the family.

The mother who progresses from anxiety and tension to a quiet, more stable personality will see maturing in her children. The father who pays more attention to the little things his children enjoy finds new companionship with his family. The parents who recognize their spiritual needs find balance and strength coming into their family.

We have seen unity emerge out of deep confusion in troubled homes. Regardless of the degree of chaos, there is hope for the family.

CHAPTER 8

GODS WITHOUT HOPE

The first time I saw Laurie was when I saw her framed in the doorway of the ranch dining hall. She looked to be in her late twenties. The setting sun, glowing red on the mountain behind her, cast an eerie light on her long, black hair. As she stood there motionless, she reminded me of a wary deer who might have wandered out of the woods and wasn't quite sure whether to come in or to run away.

The ranch hostess came to our table and asked if she could seat a guest with us. "She has never been here before—just happened to drop by."

My doctor friend and I were vacationing at Young Life's Silver Cliff Ranch in Colorado, and most of the guests had been there before. It was unusual for a casual traveler to stop in. I learned after dinner how Laurie had "happened" to appear that evening. As we helped her get settled in her cabin, she told us in a quick, matter-of-fact manner that she had recently returned from Europe and had been on her way to Aspen to play her French horn. She decided she was too tired to perform so she cancelled her engagement. Driving down the road, she saw the sign, "Silver Cliff Ranch" and spontaneously took the fork toward the Ranch. She said she was very tired and wanted to spend a few days resting "away from it all." In spite of her friendly manner, there was a lonely look in Laurie's eyes and she seemed both sad and anxious.

With her luggage, Laurie had a pile of impressive looking books. I remarked about them and she told me she was trying to find a religion that was right for her. "I'm looking into the different religions of the world."

As I looked more closely at the stack of books, I observed, "There's one missing." As soon as the words were out I felt how trite and stupid they sounded. But Laurie quickly got the point and said, "The Bible? Oh, I was brought up on that! It just isn't relevant. I found no reality in Christianity. There has to be something more." I could sense how depressed and almost hopeless she felt.

Here was a weary, tired spirit, but in spite of her obvious discouragement Laurie was determinedly searching for an answer to her restlessness.

The next morning after breakfast she pulled me aside and in a half angry, half puzzled manner asked, "What kind of a place is this?" A prayer had been said at the meal, and it was evident to Laurie that there was something different about the guests.

"Is this some sort of a religious convention?" Her voice was tense and she looked as ready to run away as she did that first evening.

It was difficult to explain the ranch to Laurie. To me, there was no place like it. It was not "religious"; there were no meetings, no schedules. It was like other high-class guest ranches. The difference was in the management and guests. Most of them—probably all—were Christians. We found the ranch restful, peaceful, and inspiring. We had chosen it as a place to fellowship with others and spend time sharing our ideas, especially in spiritual concepts. I tried to explain all of this in simple terms to Laurie.

She was visibly trembling as she said, "I'm getting out of here!" This time she did take to the woods. As she disappeared down the path, my friend joined me and I told her what had happened.

GODS WITHOUT HOPE

"I'm afraid Laurie is a very disturbed girl. We'd better see if we can help her." The thoughtful, serious tone of my friend's voice convinced me she was right; this was no simple case of religious rebellion.

We followed Laurie into the woods but could not find her, so we went to her cabin. She was not there but her things seemed untouched. Then we noticed her empty instrument case. As we walked out on the porch we heard the soft tones of a French horn coming from the woods.

We went back into the cabin and the doctor picked up a bottle of medication on the night stand and looked at the label. "It looks like we have a sick gal; she needs us both. I hope she stays," she said.

Laurie did stay. At first she said it would be only one day but it stretched out to ten. In the days that followed, Laurie joined us riding through the trails, walking down wooded paths, looking for hidden columbines, and drinking in the beauty of the mountains, and we learned something of her past. She had been dissatisfied for years with what she found in church and her religious studies at the university. In her frustration she had decided to look into other religions. She said it would be more comfortable to be an atheist than a nominal Christian whose faith had no meaning. "I need something that is real to me," she repeated again and again, and by the way she said those words I knew she was desperate.

Laurie's emotional disturbance echoed the story of countless others. We do not fully know how the restless frustration and deep unhappiness of unrewarded search for soul peace produces emotional illness. We know that frustration results when a person looks for reality where there is none, and when frustration extends for a long time it erupts in emotional or physical illness. The same happens to people who have lost spiritual security they once had. The feeling of the loss of God is the greatest pain mankind can suffer.

Many difficult questions confront us as we contemplate these deep issues. Why do so many spiritual seekers find so little? Why do some nominal Christians miss the reality of Christianity? Do these conditions invariably affect mental and physical health?

I am convinced that the lack of spiritual fulfillment has a profound effect on the emotions. If I did not believe this because the Scriptures teach it, I would believe it because of the experiences of people who have revealed their emptiness to me.

Countless times I have counseled with deeply troubled and ill people who have been put through all of the examinations and tests of an internist or spent months, sometimes years, with psychiatrists. Some have gone through the painful process of psychoanalysis and still remain ill. As one new patient said to me, "I am a well-adjusted, physically healthy *wreck!* I am a medically scientific creation with no soul. I'm miserable!" I asked her to repeat her statement so I could write it down. Her reply was, "My God, not you too! Please don't analyze what I have said!" I assured her this was not my intention.

Conflicts regarding one's faith must be included in this book because they stand side by side with other acute problems that either cause or prolong emotional illness.

Perhaps no word is more misunderstood or used with so many connotations as "faith." Some use it in the manner of the schoolboy who said, "Faith is believing what you know to be untrue." This type of emotional exercise tries to hold on by wishful thinking to something one wants though knowing it to be unreal. For most people, faith represents a vague, indefinable value that is missing in their life, and they embark on a diligent search for it with only a slight idea of what it is. A patient once asked, "Is faith something I go pick up in a basket somewhere?" Recognizing the debatable attributes of faith, Dr. Karl Menninger lists the subject under "Intangibles" in his book *The Vital Balance*.

So restless searchers doggedly and often hopelessly

follow one philosophy or creed after another on their sincere but aimless journey, and they bear the wounds of their failures in their emotions.

I have seen different types of spiritual seekers among the patients who come to my office. Most of them are unaware that their problem is a spiritual one. They describe other areas of conflicts for treatment.

Some have little, if any, belief in the existence of God, but a restless yearning drives them on in a search for something to fill the void in their lives.

John A. was that kind of a man. He was referred to our clinic because of suicide threats. John sat hunched in my office, head in his hands and tears streaming down his face as he told his story of accumulating wealth. "I thought if I could make my wad I'd have it made. I have made so much money I have problems knowing what to do with it, and I am worse off now than ever because now I don't even have the incentive for making money. I couldn't care less."

Then there was an attractive female patient who was so depressed she said her children were the only reason she didn't commit suicide. "I lived for our club and our parties, but now they mean nothing." Both she and the miserable rich man doubted God's existence. There have been many others.

These anxious people had counted on money, success, fame, intellectual achievement, and a host of other acceptance-oriented goals to satisfy their inner hunger. Instead, they found that the more they achieved the more anxious they became. Their gods are idols without hope.

How can an inner spiritual restlessness be satisfied? St. Augustine knew. He summed it all up simply when he wrote, "*Thou hast formed us for thyself, and our hearts are restless until they find rest in thee.*"

An avowed atheist once said to me, "Whatever life is all about, it is all tied up in me—just this body. What I do or do not do is up to me and me alone. There is no power outside of my own power, and I have to operate on it."

CAN I HOPE AGAIN?

"How are you doing?" I asked.

"Lousy! But God knows I am not a weak person. I have will power!"

Three times in our conversation this man referred to God, yet he insisted God did not exist. When I asked him about this, his answer was, "Oh, everybody believes in some sort of power, creator, or God—whatever you want to call it. I just don't believe he has any connection with me."

I find often that most avowed atheists do not deny a Supreme Power but rather a personal God. They believe that God may have created us, then went off and left us to our own devices. But it makes better sense to me that a Creator would expect to be in union with his creature. Patients are often amazed when I tell them I believe we were not intended to operate on our own power, and because we attempt this, confusion enters the scene and we feel lost.

An increasing number of psychiatrists and others working in related fields are accepting the proposition that man's sense of relationship to God has a profound effect on his mental health. Those interested in psychosomatic illnesses are admitting the importance of a patient's spiritual faith in the treatment of his physical symptoms.

A psychiatrist called me regarding a patient he had seen regularly for two years. She had been advised by a Christian friend to seek help from someone who could understand her spiritual conflicts. She had asked her psychiatrist about this and he had no objections to her coming to me. After several sessions in which we discussed her "turning her back on the idea of God," she said she never wanted to go back to the psychiatrist. I suggested this was not the proper way to terminate the treatment and she should talk it over with him. He called me after their subsequent conference.

"I don't understand what you do over there," he said. "I only know this patient has had an amazing recovery and I had nothing to do with it." His attitude was affable but puzzled.

"On the contrary," I answered, "your therapy removed some deep-seated blocks which made it possible for her to face her spiritual battles."

I have never met this psychiatrist face to face, but we have had long telephone conversations and he has referred other patients to me.

I wonder what his reaction might have been to my research paper described in Chapter 2—"The Role of Religion in Illness." Perhaps I should have sent it to him.

I believe he might have agreed with some who say this effect is simply the power of positive thinking rather than the action of a personal God who promised in the Scripture: "I will never leave thee nor forsake thee."* They ask, "Why should a Christian be immune?"

God does not promise Christians immunity—but rather *unity.* He does not promise the believer he will not go through illnesses and trials; he promises to go through them with him. I like the analogy of the Israelites going through the Red Sea: God did not take them around the sea or over the sea but safely through the waters—and he went with them.

It is this kind of experience that is present in real faith in God, and the faith that lacks unity with God is not true faith. Human unity with God is the missing link; without it, restlessness persists, causing illness of the person.

We often see another spiritual seeker who is more aware of his need. He believes in God, he goes to church, and he participates in the rituals honoring him. This person wants the benefits of God's approval, but he tries to force God into his own mold. He is actually ignorant of the true God, his love, his person, and his holiness. He tries to take short cuts to acceptance as our friend Bud did. He does not genuinely know Jesus Christ, so he cannot know God. It is that simple. He, too, is spiritually sick, force-feeding a pseudo-faith that is without life.

---

* *Hebrews 13:5*

As Laurie put it, "It would be better to be an atheist!" Laurie's own search was ahead of the unbeliever's and the pseudo-believer's, but she was still going in circles. Laurie's search, however, continued beyond the mountains of Colorado.

The hours of discussion in the Colorado mountains went with her to her home city. Step by step Laurie was led on a straight course from a meaningless faith in God to a personal commitment to Jesus Christ which opened up a whole new world to her in her complete person. Depression, frustration, and emotional and psychosomatic symptoms were alleviated as she was freed from the grip of guilt.

All of the knowledge Laurie had gained from her searching and her books could not lead her to God—because there was a tremendous block: guilt. Only confession and acceptance of Jesus Christ the guilt-bearer could remove that block.

Laurie's sensitive personality and tremendous energy were channeled into her new life in Christ and her spiritual growth was phenomenal. As I think of Laurie, the chain of human help impresses me. There were the understanding staff members at the Young Life ranch; a dear friend of mine, Mini Jane Johnston of the Christian Women's Clubs who "just happened" to be in Laurie's home city to visit her when Laurie arrived home angry from her Colorado confrontation; the church she found; the Bible college...the list could go on.

There have been so very many others who were searching, who were ill because they could not advance beyond a vague belief in God. Like the god of the unbelievers, their god was also without hope. Some searchers found personal faith, some did not, some are still searching.

I have been asked by a colleague, "Why do some come to spiritual reality and others do not? The need and the searching seem just as intense and desperate. The treatment seems the same. What is missing in those who fail?"

I could not answer my friend. I have often asked those questions of myself and of God. I find satisfaction in the rather simple formula that I often use with myself and with patients when unanswerable questions are asked. There are many factors that we cannot know, but there are always a few we do know. Let's hold on to those. We know that a personal faith and contact with God is God's business. We have our human part—our link in the connecting chain. When we have done all that is within our power, faith must continue. As St. Augustine expressed it, "Without God, we cannot. Without us, God will not."

Of this I am certain: when a disturbed, searching soul does make contact with God through Christ, there is a new life within. And it is this new life which constantly energizes the kind of faith that is the core of hope.

CHAPTER 9

NO IMMUNITY FOR CHRISTIANS

There is another group of emotionally ill people who often appear to have a god without hope—yet their God is authentic. These people believe in Jesus Christ and have received his life; their contact with God is genuine and God has promised them security, peace, joy, victory—the elusive goals for which men search! Yet these people are miserable!

Miserable Christians? Two incompatible words. They should not be brought together, but some Christians manage it.

These Christian believers come very reluctantly to the counselor. Our clinic was located near a city that has an unusually high proportion of Christians, and many found their way to us because we had become known as a clinic which incorporates the spiritual concept in its treatment of the person.

Often it was an acute problem that brought them to us. Perhaps there was serious trouble in a marriage, a teenage child was in difficulty, or personal depression and anxiety became unbearable. Many of these patients started their first interview by slumping into a chair and sighing, "I should not be here; I'm a Christian."

My response was always the same: "Would you say that if you were physically ill? Why should a Christian be any more immune to emotional or spiritual illness than he is to the common cold?" Many of my patients argued, "But if a Christian has faith and he prays and really believes God can do anything, why can't he be free from these problems?"

Sometimes it helped to point out that even the Apostle Paul, with all his faith, was not always triumphant over conflict and confusion. Christians, too, lack understanding of their being a "whole person." They emphasize the spiritual nature at the expense of the emotional and physical, and then experience guilt when their all-around life fails to measure up to their expectations.

Is there no advantage, then, in being a Christian? Decidedly! The believing Christian has access to the power of God on his behalf—even unconsciously—and that power is potent. According to the Bible it is the same calibre of power that raised Jesus Christ from the dead!

Why, then, do some Christians have such difficulty with their faith? Why do they appear to have a god without hope? How can they be possessors of true faith and yet so desperately without hope at times that they become ill emotionally, spiritually, and physically?

There is much that could be written on this subject. We hear and read much about the phony Christian. I'm a little weary of this; it reminds me of the screaming protestors who decry the "Establishment" but are so busy contriving ways to protest that they have not considered positive means of correction. I agree with much of the criticism; most Christian are guilty. But I would like to get beyond the ailments to the way in which the misused faith causes illness, examine the subtlety of the illness, and give a few suggestions regarding treatment.

The psychological dynamics involved in this situation are extensive, but the effects of faith in God on our mental and physical being defies precise dissection. We know something of them, however, by experience.

The Christian's inability to derive full benefit from his faith in God is felt in his whole person. His guilt, whether true or false, takes its toll. Just as a Christian is not immune from physical and emotional illnesses, he is not immune from the effects of guilt.

Misused faith is more serious for persons who truly know God than for those who do not. I have talked with many who have experienced this condition. Whether it is caused by a neurotic emotional problem, unconfessed or continuing sin, lack of regular communion with God, or whatever, there is not peace of soul for this believer. He experiences a deep sense of failure, and with it frustration, disappointment, and depression. This seems to be faith without hope. These words are a contradiction, for "Faith is the substance of things hoped for."* Can these conflicting propositions be reconciled?

Let's look at the dangers of a faith misused by the Christian. What do we do with our faith, and what is it supposed to do for us? We are told that faith just the size of a mustard seed will "move mountains." Faith has closed lions' mouths, wrought miracles, subdued kingdoms, obtained promises, and made men whole. We are told that we can use faith by trying it out, and the more we use it the stronger it will become. We picture the possibility of a strong, inner bulwark built by freedom from guilt, a strength that withstands temptations, and evidence in our lives of the fruit of the Spirit—love, joy, peace, patience, gentleness, goodness, faith, meekness, and self-control. Is it any wonder that our expectations from faith are high?

What if our faith does not bring these results? What if, instead, we experience failures, our inner weaknesses eat at us, and our energy is expended on shoring up a facade? In our effort to protect our false image we even project our defects onto others and gain solace by criticizing them. Can we see the subtlety of this? How many seekers after God are

---

* *Hebrews 11:1*

turned away from Christ by this psychological and spiritual aberration of Christians!

What does this dishonesty do to us—the real us? We may fool others and sometimes ourselves, but we know we cannot fool God. We cannot tolerate what we are and we are caught up in the practice of a faith we don't feel. Are we then so different from the searching soul who is living a meaningless existence? Can we see that though we have spiritual life we may be sicker than the person who has no life? Whether we call it imbalance, repression, guilt complex, or whatever, the condition is much the same as that of any emotionally or mentally ill patient.

Countless reasons could be given for this illness in the Christian. There is a long list of possible psychological explanations and probably a longer list of spiritual ones, but I have found *three basic causes* for this condition in Christian: *a neurotic emotional problem; unconfessed or willful sinning; lack of regular communion with God.* At the risk of oversimplifying an extremely involved problem, I shall group the patients I have seen under these three causes. In some cases two or three of these causes were involved.

There is no doubt that many devout believers have psychological problems. Some are neurotic, and some are more deep-seated. The treatment is often difficult, and it takes the combined and concentrated efforts of a psychiatrist and a spiritual counselor to produce progress. Sometimes the efforts are unconsciously sabotaged by the patient's habit of spiritualizing concepts. That is easy and comfortable for him because he has Scripture portions on the tip of his tongue. He understands biblical promises but not psychological concepts. Whenever he feels guilty, for example, he assumes a spiritual remedy is required. He does not know that his sense of guilt may be false and it must be removed in a different way.

I am often asked the question, "How can guilt be false?" Perhaps a simple illustration will suffice.

NO IMMUNITY FOR CHRISTIANS

A teen-aged girl who was a professing Christian came to our clinic. She felt so guilty much of the time that her self-image was damaged. She felt worthless to others and to herself. After hours of counseling, two types of guilt came to light.

Raised by a domineering, perfectionist mother, the daughter never felt she could do anything that was acceptable. The feeling of guilt at not achieving her mother's goals became an emotional pattern for all relationships. She felt inadequate and thus insecure. This was false guilt.

Then the daughter learned there was one thing she could do that made her feel accepted and wanted—participate in illicit sex. As she became involved with one boy after another, her need of acceptance grew instead of diminishing and her insecurity became more acute. Her false guilt drove her into a way of life that produced true guilt. In therapy, the true guilt was much simpler for her to understand and to deal with than her false guilt.

For this girl, the emotional blocks could be removed when she was able to accept psychological interpretations and cooperate with the counselor. Then when she exercised her faith realistically, progress was quick and solid.

I remember when Marie came to us for help. She was so ill emotionally she could no longer cope with her home or her children. Marie was suffering from deep-seated guilt, both true and false. Her false guilt stemmed from a lifelong complex from trying to compete with her older sister. She wanted to get well, but she was so compulsive she kept trying to use Scripture verses in a magical way. She had one for every situation. During conferences where Marie felt the security of therapeutic involvement, she would become quite realistic, but as soon as she went back to her home and her well-meaning but unwise Christian friends, she would regress to superficial spiritualizing.

We put her in the general hospital where we could control the situation. Marie was allowed no visitors or phone calls. We saw her daily in a combined medical, psychological, and spiritual treatment. We kept her isolated for three weeks during which time she could see only her husband, who was also receiving regular counseling.

A part of Marie's spiritual therapy involved reading and discussing the nature of God's grace and his acceptance of the belilever. After this had been thoroughly investigated, she was told, "All right, you know God has accepted you; now *accept yourself.* God has forgiven you, *forgive yourself!*" I gave her Eugenia Price's book *What is God Like?* to read. This is a book I use often with individuals as well as with groups. Marie read the chapters "Accepting Yourself As You Are" and "Accepting Christ As He Is" over and over. We had underlined it so much I had to bring a second copy.

Exactly when Marie accepted herself and was able to recognize the false guilt that had drained her for years, we do not know. It was all a part of the process. I only know I went into her hospital room one morning to find her radiant in her spirit and healed in her mind and body. Three years after Marie was dismissed from therapy, she continued to grow in her freedom of spirit and was a healthy and active person in all areas of her life.

We come now to the subject of sin in the Christian's life as a cause of failure and many times illness. The effects of sin in the Christian's life from the theological view is expounded in depth by many Bible scholars. Here we want to consider only that phase that has to do with the Christian's health.

First, let me say simply that sin in the Christian's life divides and confuses. For the Christian to be out of touch with God in one area of life and to strive to maintain contact in another is a sort of spiritual schizophrenia. This is living two lives. The person is split; he belongs to God yet he communes with evil. Such a conflict is constant and it eventually produces illness in varying degrees.

The Scriptures are very clear on this subject when they

say: "If iniquity be in thine hand, put it far away, and let not wickedness dwell in thy tabernacles. For then shalt thou lift up thy face without spot; yea, thou shalt be steadfast, and shalt not fear; because thou shalt forget thy misery, and remember it as waters that pass away....And thou shalt be secure, because there is hope."*

Paul illustrates the confusion that sin brings into the Christian's life in his Epistle to the Romans. Paul was aware of the depressions, the spirit of defeat and discouragement, that threaten the Christian. You may find his counsel in Romans 8:15: "Ye have not received the spirit of bondage again to fear..." Paul was writing about living the Christian life, the problem of dealing with sin and overcoming a "spirit of bondage."

Dr. Martyn Lloyd-Jones describes this beautifully and clearly in his chapter on "The Spirit of Bondage" in his book *Spiritual Depression* (Eerdmans). "The spirit of bondage in this type of Christian is ultimately a fear of themselves and a fear of failure...they enter into this spirit of bondage and are held down and troubled, worried and full of fears."

I have often seen Christians so confused by sins great and small that they become preoccupied with them. They then add the self-sins to their list—self-pity, self-denunciation, and humiliation, and the inevitable result is depression, defeat, and hopelessness. In their confusion they can see no way out.

When I see one involved in this kind of bondage, I am reminded of an experience from my childhood which I sometimes share with my patients.

My grandfather had horses, and every Saturday we went out to ride. As I was riding from the barn, a white chicken stood in the path and would not move. Out of curiosity, I got off my horse to see what was wrong. The chicken had her head buried in her feathers, and was picking away at herself, oblivious to all around her. At that

**Job 11:14-18a*

point, my grandfather cautioned me not to touch her, explaining she had a sickness that made her pick at herself all day and she would not move from the spot. I knew my brothers would soon come racing down the path on their horses so I built a little square of boards around the chicken and left her to her misery.

What a picture of the guilt-ridden Christian who, because he is more aware than the unbeliever, picks at himself constantly.

We see that the result of flagrant sin in the Christian's life is two-directional: it turns the Christian away from God and into himself. What a picture of faith without hope!

In treating the patient with this spiritual problem, the first step is to accept him as he is. The sinner always felt welcome in Jesus' presence, and yet Jesus left no doubt as to how he felt about the sin. Face to face with an adulteress, Jesus said, "I do not condemn you; go, and sin no more." The woman was well aware of her spiritual need. When the confused and frustrated Christian faces the forgiving Christ, his confusion is dissolved as he follows Christ's command, "Go, and sin no more."

I have found that the most common cause for emotional illness in the Christian who is not neurotic is his lack of frequent contact with God. He is out of conscious touch with his maker. The vertical lifeline from God to man is not being used.

He says he wants to follow Christ and be like him, but he hasn't taken the opportunity to know him. He wants to receive direction from God, but he pays attention to everything else. He wants peace, but he doesn't know the ingredients. It is amazing how many intelligent Christians rely on "something inside of me" for guidance. This, without vital, continuous contact with God, is nothing more than the misguided self.

I have heard some Christians claim that this "inner voice" is the Holy Spirit speaking to them, but their guidance leads them to act in a way that is completely contrary to what God says in his Word. We are all guilty of confusing our own will with God's to some degree, but Christians who have knowledge of God's directions in his Word realize it when they are wrong. The others may be in a state of self-hypnosis.

We are offered many remedies for this: put a definite time aside each day for study and prayer, read through the Bible on a schedule, give sacrificially for God's work, attend church regularly, fellowship with other Christians, and so one. I agree with all of these, but many of the sick Christians I have treated have done these things for years! The need goes far deeper than this. For me and for some Christians I know, it has meant getting beyond all formulas into a deep relationship with Jesus Christ and, through him, with God. It has meant practicing the presence of God in our innermost self. As this relationship develops, life and health flow through our being.True spirituality cannot be regimented, but true spirituality produces order and peace.

I remember a conversation years ago with the late pastor and Bible teacher, Harry A. Ironside. He was visiting in our home and I had shared with him some of my spiritual conflicts. For some years I had tried hard to follow the typical list of regulations. I had attended a Bible school where I had learned much about the Bible, but my personal relationshhip with Christ was anything but satisfying. Then a serious illness came. In spite of good doctors, my understanding husband, and many dear friends, there seemed to be no answer. It was then that I came face to face with Jesus Christ and knew that I must live moment by moment, hour by hour, with him. How quietly and naturally the daily Christian practices of reading and praying then fell into place!

Suddenly I hit a dry spot in my reading of the Scriptures, and so I asked Dr. Ironside, "What does one do when he simply does not enjoy the Word of God? I can't understand, after all I have been through and he as revealed himself in such a personal way, why I do not enjoy reading his Word!"

He patted my hand and answered, "I'll tell you what I did."

"You!" I interrupted. "You mean *you* have felt this way?" Here was one of the most devout Bible scholars I had known admitting there had been times when he didn't like reading God's Word!

"Yes, many times,"he answered. "I just kept reading, and God got through to me."

At that time, even though I had learned the meaning of a personal walk with God, I needed to apply self-discipline, and it worked with me too!

So, what are we really saying to Christians who are miserable? Since God deals differently with individuals, I would not presume to suggest a standard plan or set answer.

But this I know. Just as man was not intended to operate without contact with God, so the Christian is not meant to live in disunity with his Master.

Unbelievers worship gods with no real hope, and they are restless and empty. Some Christians worship the God of hope but misuse their faith and they feel restless and empty. To know the true God of hope and misuse that relationship is to lose the benefits of hope and incur illness. But the object of the Christian's hope is unchangeable, so there is always hope! As the writer of Proverbs expressed it, "Hope deferred makes the heart sick; but when dreams come true at last, there is life and joy."*

Proverbs 13:12, The Living Bible

CHAPTER 10

NO LONGER ALONE

As we remember the people we have met with their diverse problems, we realize they had one experience in common—they felt alone.

There was Bud in the hospital bed, restricted by weights and bars; Ann desperately attempting to go to the grocery store by herself; the lonely husband in the tavern and his tearful wife alone at home. We met a hopeless alcoholic sealed in his room with the gas turned on, and Les feeling alone in the county jail. Young Mike, walking through the snow in his bare feet, felt rejected; and Laurie, arms full of books, searched for a faith with reality.

Of all the experiences of man that cause deep suffering that of feeling alone is the hardest to bear. The loneliness seen daily in the counselor's office is no respecter of persons.

There is the wealthy society woman who plans entertainment for a hundred friends in her home, but even as she makes preparations her eyes fill with tears because of loneliness.

There is the family man who feels alone even at home. He sees his wife and children in a constellation apart from him. He is the provider, he pays the bills, he sends the children to good schools and puts them behind the wheel of the latest cars, but he stands on the outside of their lives looking in. Sometimes he goes elsewhere for companionship, only to deepen the loneliness.

We see the lonely woman who is starving for the love her children cannot give. Her husband is too busy to be aware of her hunger. For years she manages to exist for her children, then the day comes when the children are grown and gone from home and the loneliness results in serious illness.

The little boy draws close to his mother in the conference room. He puts his arm around her waist but she is rigid. Both are lonely, he because he cannot get what he needs, and she because she cannot give what she needs to give.

We could tell of many others whose lives reveal the deep inner need that was never intended to be a part of the human experience.

Just as man was not created to function apart from God, as we saw in chapter eight, so man was not created to function apart from man. The value of patients learning to relate to others has always been an important part of our treatment.

I recall my first group experience with patients about twelve years ago. There were six of us in the kitchen that morning. The weather was cold outside, but a fire burned brightly in the fireplace and we felt a cozy atmosphere as we sipped coffee and quietly looked at each other. The other five women were strangers to each other, but they had a common need. All were depressed, anxious, and confused—and each one felt alone in her suffering. Outwardly they did not appear especially different from any other group of women who might gather for coffee. Their conflicts might be present among women anywhere, but these women had decided to do something about their misery.

So far as "ground rules" for interaction, this group established some unlike any I have known since. They were few, and they were changed whenever the women felt it was necessary to accomplish their purpose. We decided we did not want to *do* anything; rather, we wanted to *become* something. We were not very sure what that was, so we first discussed the personality and its needs.

Just as we had looked at the needs of the whole person in individual conferences in the office, we discussed them together for new insights. We called ourselves the personality integration group. We read books and discussed them. Writings of Dr. Paul Tournier, Dr. Martyn Lloyd-Jones, Dr. Earnest White, Dr. Raymond L. Cramer, Eugenia Price, and many others had a part in our integration.

We learned that a meaningful relationship with other people is a fundamental need, for the person needs love, acceptance, and appreciation. We reminded ourselves that even Christ needed human contacts, for he appointed twelve that they might be with him.

The process of establishing harmony in the personality between body, mind, and spirit so that each could function in its relevant environment—the body in the material world, the mind in the realm of ideas, and the spirit in relationship to God—became a reality to these women.

We learned that total integration of the personality can be achieved only through union with God—it cannot be energized by man nor is it ever earned or won. We learned what it means to accept the gift of God offered through Christ and thus belong to God's family.

After our first series was completed, others joined the group and very quickly found their place. As we met week after week, the desire to belong was fulfilled and deep inferiority fellings gave way to self-respect. As I continued to counsel individually with these women, I watched them develop and make progress in all three areas of their personalities. I found them taking steps that they had not been able to take without the group process, as fear and panic diminished when they realized they were not alone.

One woman discovered that her acceptance in the small group was a stepping stone to other relationships—after all other therapy had failed to meet this need. Another discovered that individual differences and deficiencies were unimportant and did not lower her status. Each one of the original five and several of the others found a new relationship with God.

The personality integration group that started around the kitchen fireplace continued through the years. Though increased numbers necessitated our leaving the fireside, the unity and warmth of the sharing continued to permeate that group. It filled to capacity at each registration time, and many former members were "on call" to help whenever a lonely one needed a friend.

Other groups were born because of what we saw happen in this group. There have been alcoholic groups, married couples groups, teen-age groups, high school prep clubs, weight-problem groups, Bible study groups, and family and pastors groups.

We used psychiatrists, psychologists, and pastors from time to time to help in the various groups. Each experience convinced us afresh of the important contribution each has to make. The interaction that involves group members with each other as well as with the leaders is all a part of the group process.

It is not my purpose here to discuss group dynamics or to describe the results of group therapy, but rather to present it as one means of helping people to alleviate their deep loneliness.

"I feel that I don't belong in the group," an acutely depressed woman told me after her first group encounter. "They all seem so normal; I don't think any of them ever feel as I do."

"Why not ask them next week?" I suggested.

It was near the end of the session before she finally found the courage to ask her question. The response was immediate as one by one they described personal experiences that convinced her they knew the same depression, the same fears that were paralyzing her. She smiled a beautiful smile of relief and became one of the group.

A teen-age girl came into the office and stretched out on the carpet instead of sitting in her accustomed chair. "I like it better this way—it reminds me of the group where I don't feel so alone." This girl had fought coming to the group. She said she hated it, but she continued to come. One time she got high on drugs before attending, thinking that would help. Then Les became her friend and told her of her own experiences. The girl's fear and tension dissolved and she began to share with the others.

In our married couples group, we carefully observe our patients as we participate with a male co-therapist. This gives excellent opportunity to see men and women identify with others in their conflicts.

Afterward, patients, especially the men, will tell us in private sessions how surprised they were to discover other men fighting the same battles.

Here, as in individual session, we believe therapy must treat the complete person's complete needs. Communication and involvement that develops only the horizontal relationship is just part of the answer to man's loneliness. Regardless of the progress one makes in human relationships, man will remain an empty shell if he does not look up toward God in his search for identity. He may be a better adjusted, more balanced, and more healthy individual, but if he has no contact with God, his soul continues to restlessly seek reality.

Bud vividly illustrated this. He had no problem communicating with his fellow man; he loved people and used much of his time helping others in his AA groups. Everywhere he went he was liked and accepted—but Bud was empty inside. He was so unhappy he wondered if life was worthwhile. When he found God in Jesus Christ, Bud became a whole person.

CAN I HOPE AGAIN?

I have been asked often which comes first, the vertical relationship to God, or the horizontal one to man. I have seen it work both ways. Sometimes a person must come into contact with God to enable him by God's love to relate to men. Sometimes he must first relate to another person and then he can respond to God.

In *The Pursuit of God,* Dr. Tozer's great book that challenged Bud and the people he shared it with, we are told: "We pursue God because he has first put an urge within us that spurs us to the pursuit. 'No man can come to me,' said our Lord, 'except the Father which hath sent me draw him.' The impulse to pursue God originates with God."

I believe this, but we cannot know the methods God uses to bring this about. Nor do we need to know.

Here again, the psychological and spiritual are integrated. One patient cannot trust God because of the actions of people in his life who proved untrustworthy. He may never be able to trust God until he finds a human being he can trust. Another who had the same problem was able to trust God through reading God's Word.

Whatever the method or the sequence, it has been my experience that until one does relate to God and the vertical line of communication is opened, the man-to-man contact is limited in the quality of involvement.

As we look again at our man of today described in chapter one, we see him standing alone in the blinding light of his successes, trembling because of the fear in the self he cannot master. Must he remain there alone until he is consumed either by rampant inner forces or the deadly environment he has made?

The stories of the people in this book show that this is not man's destiny. Their sufferings and discoveries demonstrate that the way of sickness can be the way to health and wholeness.

If I did not believe this, life would hold no meaning or future. Each day would be but another futile struggle, and my only desire would be to get it over with.

Can we not see that though God uses many methods in dealing with his creation, they all begin and end with Jesus Christ? As Paul put it, "I can do all things through Christ which strengtheneth me." Can we not see that God intends us to be infused with Jesus Christ?

The searching people in this book found help through doctors, psychologists, psychiatrists, pastors and other human agents, but not until the Person of Jesus Christ was infused into their lives did they find their true identity and their restless search was ended.

You may have seen something of yourself in Bud, Ann, John, Laurie, or Les. Or your life situation may be completely different from theirs. But regardless of your problem or who you are, you can have hope.

As my patients shared their experiences with me, I became burdened for others who might be suffering from fear, anxiety, loneliness, confusion, or despair. This is why I felt compelled to write this book, hoping that some reader—perhaps you—might find the restful peace for which the human soul searches.

If these pages have encouraged you to persevere or to be patient, if you feel more peaceful or confident, if you feel alone no longer...this is good and I am glad. But if you have found these things and have not yet found the security and dynamic of Jesus Christ, the end is not yet for you. You are still searching.

What you lack is the genuine or real hope Dr. Tournier talked about in his Foreword. You will remember he pointed out that the narrow door that leads to this invincible hope is the admission of defeat for a commonplace hope...it is through the confession of despair that we find hope. And, the real hope he is talking about is a "new object, not any longer a thing-object, a thing we desire, partial, particular, passing; but a person, the person of Jesus Christ."

CHAPTER 11

EPILOGUE

From the deck of our mountain chalet I watched Dan as he walked down the stone-lined path to the road and then on down toward Christian Counseling Ministries' Chalet. Dan, 18, had just experienced a real emotional break-through in his hour session with me on the deck.

As I watched Dan's new stride, I asked myself as I had many times before, "What is it about therapy in this place that accounts for break-throughs coming so quickly, missing pieces of lives discovered and put into place and persons becoming whole?"

After twenty years of practicing psychotherapy in a busy medical clinic in the western suburbs of Chicago and now for three years in the spectacular beauty of the Rocky Mountains, I am not sure that I can answer that question fully, but I have arrived at some conclusions.

These conclusions were not made solely on the experiences of the past three years but have developed from ten years of working with troubled people in this mountain location.

In the summer of 1972, we decided to bring some of our troubled people from our Illinois practice to Colorado for enrichment and treatment. Twenty-five of our patients registered for that first five day Personal Enrichment

Conference at Trail West Lodge in Buena Vista, Colorado and twice that number the following year. The changed lives we witnessed during these conferences far exceeded our most extravagant expectations.

Jane and Tom walked down the aspen trail hand in hand, both feeling a bit strange responding to a touch they had not felt for years.

Marge and her daughter Dottie, stood side by side at the Lodge deck rail watching the shadows on Mt. Princeton. They turned and saw each other perhaps for the first time in their adult lives. Suddenly they were in each other's arms, their eyes moist with tears.

Inside, a lonely man was no longer lonely as he felt a part of those around him.

These and many others experienceing new closeness, new love and renewed fellowship with God were too occupied with their own inner excitement to note the thoughtful expressions on the faces of their leaders.

What was there about these five day conferences at Trail West that was different from the individual counseling sessions and week-end retreats at home base? Was it that, because of the previous counseling they were conditioned and thus ready to close in and put their lives together? That possibility was considered but there had been other long week-ends near home with no results comparable to these.

My doctor friend and I, who had worked together for nearly fifteen years in the treatment of the whole person took a walk in the mountains to try to analyze what was happening.

We recalled that memorable experience years before when we were in a jeep up here with Jim Rayburn, founder of Young Life, and his pointing to this spot and saying, "I think God wants a place there where people can get away from it all and find Him and themselves." It seemed so much like a vision then—and it was. But it had come true. Here was the luxurious Trail West Lodge, the surrounding

Trail West Village with lovely chalets nestled among the pine trees and there was no doubt that God's Spirit was here.

We decided that a combination of all of these factors gave the answer to the spectacular and beautiful results we were witnessing in the lives of the Conference participants.

It was then that we were convinced that chalets were needed where these troubled people could stay longer and receive more intensive help. In 1978 CCM was incorporated as a non-profit organization and a chalet in Trail West Village was purchased. Since the day it was dedicated, individuals, couples and families have come from all over the country to receive counseling.

Now, after those years of experiences with conference participants (we continue to schedule two or three a year) and the past three years of working with CCM's Chalet guests I have some conclusions which might partially explain what is happening.

Here, in the mountains one is completely removed from environmental stress. He is away from the person or persons who may be involved with his problems—or from his office, boss or whatever. He lives with others and has the opportunity to relate to the "family" in a therapeutic way. This often serves as a stepping stone to finding his comfortable place in society.

Often, there are therapy sessions while walking through the woods, sitting on a rock or an old log, or on the Chalet deck that overlooks the valley and the mountains. I shall never forget a session when a party of four were climbing to the top of Mt. Antero—over 14,000 ft. Two of us stopped to breathe—the air was thin—and we were exhausted but the peak was not too far away. Our experienced leader and his wife were a few yards ahead. There was a sheer drop and our midwestern friend panicked. So, with two gals stretched out on a barren rock there was a brief therapy session that brought results and we reached the top!

CAN I HOPE AGAIN?

Since Chalet I is a year round ministry, the mountains in the winter also bring spectacular beauty into the therapy experience. My Counseling office opens to the deer path that comes down from the National Forest. Often deer are feeding just a few feet away. There is skiing, cross country as well as on the slopes. For some, just walking under the shadow of snow covered peaks against a deep blue sky is an unforgettable experience.

Just how all of this comes together to bring more lasting results more quickly may be summed up in one 21 year old boy's statement. His words came out of deep loneliness and hurting as he asked, "Why is it my mother tells me so many people love me—even God—but I can't feel it?" He then went on to answer his own question. "It is—it must be—something in me. But, out here I am beginning to feel. I feel the mountains, the woods, you, the friends around and—especially God. I really think *I feel loved.*"

So, if I would attempt to put my evaluation into one statement it would be: The freedom for troubled people to accept the love of others, of God and finally, of self.

Living in the beauty of God's creation blocks are often removed, giving freedom to accept the love of God of others and then of self.

Questions are sometimes asked, "Does it last?" What happens when they leave? If the Chalet I therapy only helped people to experience love—as tremendous as that is—lasting results would be limited. The Chalet I guest encounters God. He not only experiences His love which often must comes first, but he is helped to explore his relationship with Christ on a realistic Biblical level. He learns the beauty of true meditation where he allows God to speak to him and he comes to realize the privilege and importance of a daily walk with Christ.

Follow up contacts with former guests reveal that what was started in the mountains continues to be effective at home.

EPILOGUE

After trying traditional therapy for years, an alcoholic spent three weeks at the chalet before Christmas and has remained dry ever since. When asked how he explained the difference in the chalet therapy from the office therapy in the city, he replied—"It's the place, the tremendous beauty of God's creation—it helped me to get back into relationship with God and then the deer—the innocent beauty of the deer—did something for me." And then he looked at me hesitatingly and said, "I also see a renewed therapist." That is true. I like me better out here.

There was the response from the husband whose wife came to a conference and stayed on at Chalet I—"I don't know just what happened out there but it was tremendous and I want to come and see for myself."

The reactions could go on and on both from Conferences and from Chalet I.

You may wonder where these people come from? How do they know about the ministry?

Many have come from contacts during twenty years of practice in Illinois, Some learned of the chalet ministry when attending one of the conferences. Still others were referred by pastors, physicians, or other professionals.

One nationally-known psychiatrist wrote in a letter to other professionals:

> "The purpose of Chalet I is to treat the troubled person who is not severly disturbed but needs to be relieved of environmental pressures and receive competent therapy. I know of no other comparable facility in the country that is offering this type of service in this type of atmosphere and I can recommend Chalet I with confidence and without reservation."

As I am putting the finishing touches on this book I am writing from our Colorado chalet deck and as I look out at the valley and Mt. Princeton I am reminded that more than 23 years have passed since that summer at Silver Cliff Ranch which is only a few miles away.

CAN I HOPE AGAIN?

Young Life's Trail West Lodge is now the guest Lodge and Silver Cliff is a teen ranch. It is like we have come back home.

It was during that summer at Silver Cliff—which seems so long ago and yet just yesterday—that my physician friend and I shared our concepts and decided to work together. Sometimes, I think all of those years of working with troubled people was a preview—a preparation for our Mountain Ministry now.

Last winter, we were asked to open an extension of CCM in Florida. The Florida "extension" department that ended so abruptly the day that Bud went out to sea is now back in operation!

Our experiences and the experiences of those we have worked with have shown us over and over that with God's help and promise, we can hope again—no matter how hopeless a situation may seem.